0700035

D0095857

THE
SUPERMAN
HANDBOOK

THE ULTIMATE GUIDE
TO SAVING THE DAY

By Scott Beatty

Foreword by Mark Waid

Pencils by John Delaney

Inks by Dave Cooper and Terry Beatty

Colors by Mike Rogalski

Superman created by Jerry Siegel and Joe Shuster

QUIRK BOOKS
PHILADELPHIA

Visit DC Comics online at www.dccomics.com or at keyword DCCOMICS on America Online.

Library of Congress Cataloging in Publication Number: 2005936990

ISBN: 1-59474-113-1

Printed in Singapore

Typeset in Futura, Magnesium, and Serpentine

Designed by Michael Rogalski

Distributed in North America by Chronicle Books
85 Second Street
San Francisco, CA 94105

10 9 8 7 6 5 4 3 2 1

Quirk Books
215 Church Street
Philadelphia, PA 19106
www.quirkbooks.com

0 1021 0210820 0

Contents

Foreword

Good news: Whether you realize it or not, you and Superman share a superpower.

Wait, it gets better: Not just *any* power.

His *greatest* power.

The legend of Superman is one of the world's best-known stories. Rocketed as an infant from the doomed planet Krypton, the alien Kal-El was adopted and raised by a kindly farm couple in the American heartland. As an adult, disguised as Clark Kent, he came to the big city of Metropolis and works today as a reporter for the *Daily Planet*. Clark's friends and co-workers think he's an ordinary, mild-mannered fellow, no different from you or me—but when danger calls, Kent slips out of sight, peels off his Oxford shirt and nonprescription eyeglasses to reveal a hidden costume, and takes to the skies as Superman, champion of the weak and the oppressed.

When I was a child, I was at first humbled by the seemingly endless array of dazzling abilities Superman wielded. He could fly, but no matter how many dishtowel capes I pinned around my neck, gravity and I maintained our master-servant relationship. Superman could see through walls, while my corrective lenses got thicker every year. Bullets bounced off his chest, whereas I'm still carrying around scars on the knees I skinned at age four. And five. And so on. And yet, despite our numerous differences, I never ceased to be impressed—genuinely awed, in fact—by the one thing he does that I find most amazing of all. Here is a guy with the power of a god, someone who can rule the world starting today if he desires. Who can have absolutely anything his heart longs for and get away with positively any deed imaginable, all without one single threat of reprisal. But with the *totality of time and space* subject to his *slightest whim*—

—he chooses only to *help others*.

That is Superman's greatest power. When presented with the opportunity, he takes action to make things better—and that's a power that lies within us all.

In the pages that follow, you'll discover all manner of techniques and tips to save the day, and you'll probably be relieved to know that none of them requires leaping over tall buildings or bending steel in your bare hands. Some of these skills consist of first-aid knowledge or advice you can use every day; others are slightly less commonly pragmatic, unless you find yourself walking past burning buildings with unusual frequency or your friends and loved ones are often chained to runaway express trains by criminal geniuses. Still, it's all good advice. Even if you are just an ordinary, mild-mannered fellow, you can never tell when you'll be called upon to answer a cry for help.

Go on. Be the hero who gets that kitten safely down from the tree.

You'll feel so good, you could fly.

Mark Waid
Los Metropolis, California

***Mark Waid** has, over the past 20 years, written several comic books a month, including tales of Superman and the Justice League, and he's not tired yet. A pro and a fan, he lives in Los Angeles in one of those apartments where it's hard to find a place to stand that doesn't have a picture of Superman in your line of sight.*

Introduction

Oh, to be Superman.

The alien infant Kal-El escaped his home planet Krypton's destruction and traveled across space to Earth, a far inferior world, devoid of the technological wonders and developmental zeniths achieved by Kryptonian civilization.

But by the time Krypton exploded from internal stresses, the planet's society had become cold and emotionless; the last act of love committed on its sterile surface was Jor-El and Lara's decision to send their only child out into the cosmos like some celestial Moses.

Kal-El zoomed out of the sky, landed in rural Kansas, and was raised by Jonathan and Martha Kent, real salt-of-the-earth folks, who taught the Last Son of Krypton that honesty and integrity are the highest virtues. They also instilled in their adopted son—whom they named Clark, Martha's maiden name—the Golden Rule of doing unto others as you would have them do unto you, a life lesson that would carry him far.

In his teens, Clark developed the first of many superpowers, abilities far beyond those of a normal man. His Kryptonian physiology, energized by the rays of Earth's yellow sun, caused Clark's skin to become invulnerable, and his strength increased a thousandfold. He soon learned he could defy gravity, flying into the stratosphere and beyond and finding himself capable of surviving in the unyielding vacuum of space and the crushing depths beneath the ocean waves. His senses became so finely tuned that he could hear sounds from more than 100 miles (160 km) away and see through virtually any substance by sheer force of will, with a kind of X-ray vision. Blessed with miraculous powers and a desire to use them to battle crime and injustice, the Man of Steel didn't just grow up to be a man. He became the paradigm for heroic perfection, a Man of Tomorrow we can all aspire to be. In short, Superman.

Unfortunately, Superman's one of a kind. Heat vision and unaided flight are not abilities you are likely to acquire, no matter how hard you try. And as a normal human being, there's no practical way to gain the strength of ten men without the use of anabolic steroids and a training regimen that would last half your lifetime.

However, there is more to Superman than superpowers and extraordinary feats. Ma and Pa Kent made sure of that. Being Superman isn't just about saving Lois Lane from certain doom or bashing Lex Luthor and his ilk into sub-mission (though, in the case of super-villains such as Luthor, it might be useful to know how to deliver a knockout punch; see page 13). First and foremost, being Superman is about doing right by your fellow men and women. If you aspire to the same ideals of honesty and integrity as Superman, doing the right thing and becoming the ultimate good guy can run the gamut from the high heroics of rescuing someone who's drowning to unsung but noble deeds such as refilling your office water cooler without being asked.

Collected here are real-world tips on how to become a real-life Superman. Consider this a primer on doing the right thing under circumstances both dire and mundane. With this knowledge, you'll not only earn the respect of the people you help, but you'll also be a *superman* in the eyes of the world's greatest hero, an orphan who made Earth his home. If you've got the will to do good, turn the page.

Chapter 1

Super-Skills

You don't have to have superpowers to be a good guy . . . but it helps.

Superman's astounding abilities don't make him a hero. His powers (outlined on the following pages) certainly facilitate his many feats of heroism. But it's his overwhelming and unstoppable drive to help others that makes him a super hero.

Which is a good thing, because the human body is limited to some preset parameters. You can only become so strong and so fast, and you can only see so well. However, these limitations don't preclude you from acting like a hero in times of need. As you read on, you'll see that many acts of derring-do often require only two qualities in the average good guy: advance thinking and a clear head. Armed thus, anyone of modest strength faced with a dire situation can capture a bad guy or save someone from calamity. The skill sets outlined here don't require superspeed or X-ray vision—only a quick reaction time, an awareness of your surroundings, and a willingness to help others.

How to Knock Out a Villain

With an ordinary bad guy, Superman has to pull his punches. A single, untempered blow could send an opponent into orbit. An innocent hand gesture could register as a knockout blow to the average thug. Of course, Superman's faced off against much worse. The super-villain Mongul, leader of Warworld and its deadly interstellar gladiator games, is actually even stronger than Superman. Luckily, Superman was able to hone his powers in Mongul's arena and eventually bested the alien tyrant. By following some of the basics of boxing, you too can take on a worthy opponent and send him into slumberland.

Step 1: Set up your opponent with a light jab.
Boxing is often a well-choreographed dance, as fighters dodge and weave in search of an opening to land the perfect punch. Begin by setting up your opponent with a light jab to his face, aiming for the eyes or nose. A blow to either area will cause his eyes to water, temporarily blinding and disorienting him. The jab will throw him off his game, forcing him into a retreat or leaving him open for additional blows.

Step 2: Follow with several quick jabs to the body.
Quick punches to a villain's chest or torso will force your opponent to lower his guard. Like most boxers—or anyone engaged in a fistfight—your opponent will be concerned with protecting his head. The quick jabs at his torso will trick him into thinking that you're now only concerned with punching low.

Step 3: When your opponent drops his guard, spring up fast with an overhand cross.
When your opponent drops his arms to protect his torso, spring up with an overhand cross and strike him squarely at ear level between his ear and his temple. A cross is one of the most devastating blows and will disorient him, if not render him briefly unconscious. This blow often results in a "flash knockdown," a delayed

Superman begins with a light jab, aiming for Mongul's eyes and nose.

Superman follows with rapid punches to the torso.

As Mongul drops his guard, Superman hits him with a left cross.

Superman finishes Mongul off with a right hook.

How to Knock Out a Villain   15

reaction where the person struck doesn't realize that he has been hit so hard. He's likely to stagger a few feet before falling down and seeing stars.

 While most assume that a straight-on shot to the face is more stagger-ing, a shot to the side of the head strains blood vessels and nerve endings. When you make his head spin with that right cross, increased rotational forces stretch the vessels and endings, causing your opponent to lose consciousness.

Step 4: Finish with a hook.

If your overhand punch doesn't do the job completely, finish your opponent off with a right or left hook to score the knockout. Thus, the overhand-hook combo is a one-two punch—and spells lights out for your opponent!

SUPERMAN'S SUPER-ABILITIES

Before you can imitate Superman, you have to know Superman. Pity the super-villain who assumes that the Man of Steel is merely super-strong and able to fly. He has a few other tricks up his blue sleeves, skintight as they may seem. Taken individually or en masse, Superman's abilities make him far superior to the average human being. They're enough to make him a walking weapon of mass destruction. Thank goodness he's on *our* side! All of Superman's abilities are fueled by Earth's yellow sun (as opposed to Krypton's red dwarf), which energizes his Kryptonian cellular structure as if he were a living solar battery. Here's a thorough rundown of Superman's awesome powers:

Superstrength
The limits of his superstrength have never been tested, but Superman has lifted mountains and moved the moon from its orbit on more than one occasion. In his super-strong grip, he's pressed a lump of coal into a flawless diamond. And with that same super-strong fist, the Man of Steel has punched super-villains right off the surface of the planet and into orbit. His great strength is matched by equally tireless stamina.

Invulnerability
Thanks to Earth's sun and his unique Kryptonian physiology, Superman generates an invisible force field around his entire body. This aura is barely a micron in thickness, permitting you to touch him. Bullets, death rays, and other threats, however, bounce right off his skin. He's been at ground zero for nuclear explosions of 40 megatons (36 million metric tonnes) or more and suffered almost no ill effects, and he's even successfully withstood the space-time warping produced by close proximity to a black hole, whose gravity is stronger than any other force in the universe.

Flight
Whether leaping a tall building in a single bound or flying nonstop from Metropolis to Tokyo in minutes, Superman is unfettered by Earth's gravitational pull. He can also fly through the vacuum of space at velocities that have yet to be measured. He isn't faster than light, but Superman has rocketed at speeds close to it.

Super-Vision

Superman's super-vision can be broken down into several distinct powers, limited only by the speed at which light travels.

X-Ray Vision: His most famous ocular ability, Superman's X-ray vision enables him to see through virtually any substance; only extremely dense materials, such as lead, can block his gaze.

Heat Vision: Shooting out like twin red laser beams from his eyes, Superman's heat vision varies in intensity from a warming glow to the heat of a sun.

Microscopic Vision: With microscopic vision, Superman can observe even the tiniest detail, even to the edges of the subatomic realm.

Telescopic Vision: Superman's telescopic vision enables him to discern even very distant objects with 20/20 clarity.

Super-Breath

Superman's lung capacity is staggering. By super-inhalation, he can condense vast amounts of air in his lungs, pressurizing it into a super-cold state. This enables him to extinguish raging infernos with a concentrated super-exhalation. He can also hold his breath much longer than any human being, making it possible for him to survive for extended periods in the airless expanses of space or far below the surface of the oceans.

Superspeed

Superman isn't known as the Fastest Man Alive. That nickname belongs to the Scarlet Speedster known as the Flash, who can move at velocities approaching the speed of light (thanks to his ability to tap into an interdimensional field called the Speed Force). Superman's incredible celerity is powered by his solar-charged cells. Naturally, everyone has long wondered who is faster, the Man of Steel or the Scarlet Speedster. On several occasions, the heroes have engaged in a footrace over land, across the seas, and through space and time to settle the question once and for all. Each time, however, something has prevented the match from being a fair test. But Superman is, at worst, the second fastest man alive—which is still pretty speedy.

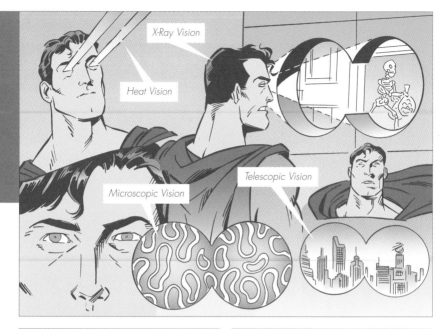

How to Break Through a Door

To gain entry into a super-villain's secret sanctum, Superman can knock down most doors with the flick of one super-strong finger. But even Superman has met doors he couldn't best; Lex Luthor's LexCorp building in Metropolis was famously impervious to the Last Son of Krypton. Even without super-strength, you can root out bad guys from their hideouts and make a fast and spectacular entrance by exploiting structural weaknesses in most standard doors. Your primary tool will be your foot. Ramming the door with your shoulder or body exerts far less force than a well-placed kick.

Step 1: Determine how much force will be required.

Assess the door, and determine how much force you'll need to apply. Generally speaking, the heavier the door, the harder you'll have to kick. Tap the door to find out if it's hollow or solid. Many modern interior doors have a hollow core and may respond quickly to a determined kick, but older homes tend to have solid wood doors. Most exterior doors, whether in new or old homes, will be solid wood or have a solid core.

Step 2: Find the "sweet spot."

Locate the point on the door where the door's latch meets the frame. If it's an interior door, the door's lock and latch may be part of the same mechanism. If it's an exterior door, look for a dead-bolt security lock, usually located above the door's latch mechanism. An exterior door's latch mechanism will likely not lock—it is the dead bolt you need to kick.

Step 3: Kick!

With the heel of your foot, kick the lock mechanism. For greatest impact, it's important that you direct your kick as close to the lock as possible. If the door is made of lightweight or thin wood, one kick will break through. Thicker doors may require several kicks.

Alternative Method: The Right Tools

If your kicks aren't working or you have time to retrieve your toolbox from your basement or car, the right tools can make all the difference.

Screwdriver: Some bedroom or bathroom doors have an emergency access hole in the center of the door. This allows entry to the locking mechanism. By inserting a screwdriver or thin probe, you should be able to turn or push the mechanism and open the lock.

Flathead Screwdriver and Hammer: Remove the door's hinges by placing the screwdriver's head underneath a hinge and striking the handle with a hammer. Make sure the screwdriver's head touches the end of a bolt or screw securing the hinge to the door.

Crowbar: Insert the crowbar between the lock and the door, and wrench the lock off the door by prying back and forth. Alternatively, use the crowbar to pry the hinges off the door.

Alternative Method: Steel Ram

Powerful, well-placed kicks will usually do the trick, but repeated boots to a stubborn door can cost you the element of surprise. Or you could kick right through a thin door and find your foot caught in the hole. Most cops use steel rams—some one-handed, others requiring several handlers—weighing 20 pounds (9 kg) or more to bash against door handles and locks. A single ram wielder will break down the door; you can then step away to allow armed officers to enter. Advance planning is required—you will need to locate a ram or similar tool and store it nearby for emergency use, and possibly recruit a friend or two to help wield the ram.

Alternative Method: Jaws of Life

Firefighters use the so-called Jaws of Life to dismantle crashed vehicles and free accident victims. The hydraulic prying action of this high-powered pneumatic tool makes short work of twisted metal. Law enforcement officers employ the Jaws of Life to tear doors off their jambs, allowing them to kick them down in short order. Because of its speed and effectiveness, this method facilitates the element of surprise. However, since this technique requires planning to track down the equipment and help from like-minded good guys, it's not likely to serve you in a pinch.

How to Tackle a Runaway Goon

The Man of Steel doesn't have much to worry about when it comes to apprehending ordinary criminals, although he has his own rogues' gallery of bad guys who are capable of putting up a serious fight (check some of them out on page 26). Luckily, you're much more likely to encounter a normal thug than you are Bizarro or Darkseid. And for the average good guy, tackling such a thug requires only sprinting speed and courage—although sometimes a little bit of teamwork with a fellow crime fighter can be a real help.

Step 1: Cut the distance.
In a footrace with a fleeing criminal, your first task is to close the gap between the two of you. The person you're chasing has fight-or-flight instincts toggled directly to flight, and if nabbed, he'll fight with adrenaline-fueled desperation to get away. Try to cut the distance without telegraphing your intent to tackle him, lest he duck out of the way and leave you gripping pavement instead of his criminal coattails. Do your best to stay out of his line of sight if he turns around to see you; this way, you can maintain an element of surprise.

Step 2: Tackle.
If you're alone, grab him around the middle from behind, pinning his arms to his sides with your grasped arms. With your weight, push him forward and to the ground, releasing your grip just long enough to get his arms behind his back. If you're pursuing with a partner, tackling is a little easier—one of you grabs his upper body while the other trips him and grabs his legs. Forward momentum should send the villain crashing to the ground. You can also grab one of the villain's shoulders and force him to the ground facedown for cuffing.

Step 3: Lock his arms with a wrist bar, arm bar, or other joint-locking technique to keep him from fighting you.
The simplest hold, a wrist bar, is applied by grasping the bad guy's wrist, applying pressure against the back of his hand with your thumb, and bending it back

Superman applies a wrist bar hold to keep Bizarro down for the count.

toward his arm. The move immobilizes his hand and causes him increasing pain with added pressure.

Step 4: Pin him.
Once the bad guy is facedown on the ground, with his head turned to the side so that he can breathe unhindered, pin him by placing your knee on the small of his back. Your weight alone will keep him pinned, especially if you secure both his arms behind him with his thumbs pointed inward so that he cannot get any leverage to roll out from under you or lift himself up. A knee on his neck will also work, leaving the criminal more concerned with catching his breath than fighting his way free.

Step 5: Identify yourself as one of the good guys.
Once he knows he's nabbed, your criminal is likely to realize that further action will only exacerbate the situation.

Step 6: Search for weapons.
Once the culprit is securely pinned, search him quickly for any weapons he might potentially use against you, and then put cuffs on him, if you have a pair, and wait for the authorities to arrive.

MOST WANTED: SUPERMAN'S GREATEST FOES

For Superman, being the ultimate good guy isn't just a matter of performing heroic deeds and protecting the innocent from natural disasters. Unfortunately, the Man of Steel finds that the greatest difficulty in saving people is getting past a whole host of super-villains who are actively putting people in danger; sometimes their modus operandi is to put the public at risk to draw Superman into a fight. Here are some of the major villains who get in Superman's way regularly. As you use this book to make a name for yourself, be sure to keep an eye out for your own Lex Luthor or Bizarro.

Lex Luthor

The former Metropolis mogul and CEO of LexCorp is a genius, but his megalomania has given him an insatiable hunger for power and has made him incredibly jealous of Superman's superpowers. Luthor has gone so far as to run for and win the U.S. presidency, and he uses his position as the most powerful man in the Western world to enact diabolical revenge schemes against the Man of Steel. Lex will stop at nothing, including razing Metropolis, to see Superman destroyed.

Metallo

Small-time thug John Corben would have died in a car crash if not for the intervention of Professor Emmett Vale. Vale was a genius in the field of robotics, and he erroneously believed that Superman was an alien robot and a threat to humanity. So instead of simply saving John Corben, he transplanted Corben's brain into a robot made of a super-strong alloy called metallo, with an especially potent power source—a two-pound (.9 kg) chunk of kryptonite, giving the newly christened Metallo a heart that's poisonous to the Man of Steel. Ever since he thoughtlessly rewarded Dr. Vale by murdering him, Metallo has developed a number of new abilities, including the power to absorb any metal into his robot body, making him nigh indestructible!

Darkseid

Dreaded ruler of the hellish planet Apokolips, Darkseid has a physical strength on par with Superman's, but his most feared power is the Omega Effect. Fired from his eyes, Omega Beams have a number of capabilities, including completely disintegrating their target. Darkseid has an almost philosophical belief in his own supremacy and is constantly seeking the Anti-Life Equation, which he sees as the means to control all sentient life in the universe. The possibility that the Equation is to be found somewhere on Earth regularly puts Darkseid at direct odds with Earth's greatest defender, Superman.

Brainiac

When the alien Vril Dox tried to take control of his home planet, Colu, he was discorporated and scattered across space. Reconstituted as a floating consciousness with a computer-like intelligence and rechristened as the villainous Brainiac, he found his way to Earth, where he became one of Superman's most persistent foes, upgrading his computer mind again and again into different forms in an ongoing attempt to conquer Earth.

Mr. Mxyzptlk

His consonant-heavy surname is pronounced "Mix-yez-pit-lick," and he is Superman's weirdest enemy (stealing the title from Bizarro). Mxyzptlk hails from a five-dimensional world called Zrfff, where science is so advanced it resembles unpredictable magic. He enjoys coming to Earth simply to torment Superman with super-tricks that often bend reality in ways that he finds amusing and others find horrifying. The only way to return Mxyzptlk to Zrfff is to trick him into saying, spelling, or writing his name backward: *Kltpzyxm!* Once he's been tricked, Mxyzptlk can't return for 90 days.

Mongul

Ruler of the star-roving mechanized Warworld, Mongul once captured the Man of Steel and pitted him against equally formidable combatants in Warworld's gladiatorial arena. When Superman would not yield to Mongul's demands to slay his opponents, Mongul challenged the Man of Steel himself in the ultimate grudge match. Superman escaped Mongul's clutches and later fought the tyrant on Earth, when he attempted to re-create it as a new Warworld (destroying scenic Coast City in the process). Mongul's son, also named Mongul, and his daughter, Mongal (Mongul is not known for his originality), have also become enemies of Superman.

Mr. Mxyzptlk, imp from the Fifth Dimension

Mongul, master of Warworld

Lex Luthor, megalomaniacal genius

Metallo, powered by kryptonite

Toyman

Toymaker Winslow Schott was a victim of corporate downsizing when Lex Luthor's LexCorp conglomerate gobbled up Schott's toy company. At first, this vengeful Toyman took out his aggressions by trying to kill Luthor; his creations were so ingenious he was hired to build weapons for the crime group known as Intergang. Later, an increasingly unhinged Toyman targeted Metropolis's children for tragedy, thus pitting Superman against Schott's weaponized toys. Schott's creations are a reminder that even the cutest wind-up toy can be a deadly weapon.

General Zod

For plotting sedition on planet Krypton, the military genius General Zod was sentenced to life imprisonment within the Phantom Zone, a limitless region of limbolike space discovered by Superman's biological father, Jor-El. In his many years trapped wraithlike in the Zone, Zod watched Krypton's destruction and plotted revenge against Jor-El's only son, eventually escaping and battling Superman on Earth, where the evil general found himself gifted with the very same powers as the Man of Steel. Fortunately, Superman's years of experience aided him in defeating Zod, who remains a foe determined to destroy the House of El.

Parasite

Janitor Rudy Jones was transformed by strange radiation at S.T.A.R. Labs into the monstrous and purple-skinned Parasite, who can absorb the memories and abilities of any living creature he touches—while draining them of life. He's become an especially powerful foe for Superman; the Man of Steel can't fight him without the risk of Parasite absorbing his powers.

Doomsday

This super-foe succeeded where all others in Superman's rogues' gallery could not: He killed the Man of Steel. Created by the rogue alien geneticist Bertron on Krypton many millennia ago, Doomsday has an invulnerable hide covered in sharp, bony protrusions. He was bioengineered to evolve constantly and never truly be killed; countless deaths have purged him of any weakness, making him essentially unstoppable. He first appeared in a deadly rampage across Earth that ended with Superman and Doomsday apparently killing each other on the streets of Metropolis. Fortunately, the Man of Steel returned from the dead . . . but so did Doomsday, now evolved into an even greater super-villain.

Bizarro

One of Superman's most strange and colorful villains, Bizarro is more misunderstood than misanthropic. Still, this imperfect duplicate of Superman is a super-threat because he has all of Superman's strength but none of Superman's sanity. In Bizarro's twisted mind, everything is turned into its opposite; he lives in a world of antonyms and bad diction. Thus, "evil am good!" Fitting this theme, some of Bizarro's powers are backward: He has cold vision instead of Superman's heat vision, and he can exhale flame instead of the Man of Steel's super-cold breath. It's his abuse of language that really upsets grammarians, however.

BAD ENGLISH: HOW TO SPEAK BIZARRO

Bizarro World, sometimes called Htrae, is cube-shaped and a decidedly odd place to visit. Following the Bizarro logic that good is bad and bad is good, Superman himself was imprisoned there for the crime of being normal. So if you're planning a trip there, it's even more important than usual to learn the local language. Here are some simple rules of grammar you should keep in mind when attempting to converse with Bizarro and his people.

Rule 1: Substitute the pronoun *me* for *I* in all speech. The personal pronouns *he* and *she* should be replaced with *him* and *her*, respectively. Essentially, Bizarro-Speak—at its core—is baby talk for adults.

Rule 2: *Am* should be substituted for all *to be* verb tenses (*is, are,* etc.). Or you can just mix up verb tenses each time for the Bizarro effect.

Rule 3: Double negatives (*no nothing,* etc.) are completely appropriate and should be randomly and frequently inserted into otherwise normal sentences.

Rule 4: The meaning of Bizarro sentences is often the opposite of what is intended: *Bad* is *good, down* is *up,* and *happy* is *sad.*

Rule 5: Exclamations should be reversed, with negative exhortations substituted for positive ones and vice versa—but not always. If you speak in opposites with total consistency, you would be much easier to understand—and that would be bad.

Rule 6: Frequently begin sentences with "Bah!"

Rule 7: Laugh inappropriately with a hearty "ha-ho!" when the situation would otherwise call for sympathy.

And remember the Bizarro Code:
  US DO OPPOSITE OF ALL EARTHLY THINGS!
  US HATE BEAUTY!
  US LOVE UGLINESS!
  AM BIG CRIME TO MAKE ANYTHING PERFECT ON BIZARRO WORLD!

Now that you know the rules, try these simple statements on for size:

Example 1

STANDARD ENGLISH: Oh, no! We are being invaded by living blue kryptonite creatures!

BIZARRO-SPEAK: Hooray! Us am being invaded by living blue kryptonite creatures!

Example 2

STANDARD ENGLISH: Great job, Jimmy! I'm rewarding you by giving you a raise!

BIZARRO-SPEAK: Bad job, Jimmy! Me reward you by lowering your salary!

Example 3

STANDARD ENGLISH: I'm having a wonderful time!

BIZARRO-SPEAK: Me am not having terrible time!

There! Now you am not ready to speak Bizarro! Me wish you bad luck! Hello!

How to Tie Up a Henchman

Being a true hero means subduing criminals, not simply doing away with them. But if authorities aren't quick to arrive, you might tackle your bad guy only to find that a more permanent solution than sitting atop him is required. Superman has been known to bend guns into makeshift manacles to bind the arms of henchmen, thereby disabling them and their weapons in one easy move. Easy for the Last Son of Krypton, that is; but bending steel in your bare hands is not the only fast and simple way to tie up a criminal. A pair of standard-issue steel handcuffs or nylon flex-cuffs (which are used more and more by real-life crime fighters) are, however, a requirement. These key tips for cuffing will quickly put your average criminal under wraps.

Step 1: Secure the arms.

A criminal should be handcuffed with his arms behind his back, thumbs inward. If he's cuffed with his arms in front, he could still strike you in any number of ways, or even use the cuffs as a garrote to choke the life from you. With his thumbs to the inside, he will be unable to gain leverage.

Step 2: Apply handcuffs or flex-cuffs to one hand.

Handcuffs are particularly effective because they ratchet closed tightly and can be double-locked so that the criminal cannot rotate his wrists inside the cuffs or slip through the steel bands. Flex-cuffs, hardened nylon strips, are snug restraints, ratcheting tighter as they're pulled taut. Handcuffs require steel keys to unfasten the locking mechanism, which can be picked if the bad guy is deft with a paper-clip or a bit of hidden wire. Flex-cuffs, on the other hand, are disposable, and you'll need special cutting tools to snip them off (or perhaps just strong teeth — some desperate criminals have been known to gnaw through the heavy nylon strips). Both options are widely used by law enforcement agents, though many swear that when their lives are on the line, only the tried-and-true steel handcuffs will do.

Step 3: Slide the cuff through a belt loop.

Even with his arms cuffed behind his back, a determined bad guy can get his hands in front of him. He first kneels and slides his bound wrists under his buttocks; then he rolls backward and lifts the cuffs over his bent legs; finally, he leaps to his feet, arms front and spoiling for a fight. To keep a step ahead of the villains, consider sliding the cuff—either steel or flex—through the rear belt loop of a bad guy's pants before cuffing him, securing the cuffs to his own clothes.

Step 4: Cuff the other hand.

Step 5: Hold him down or otherwise secure him.

Pin him by placing your knee on the small of his back as he lies on the ground. If you put him in a car or other vehicle, make sure there are no objects at hand that he could use to escape before authorities arrive.

How to Dodge Bullets

Regular bullets bounce off Superman, but even Superman has proven vulnerable to kryptonite bullets. The villain Metallo once shot the Man of Steel in the chest with one, and if Batman hadn't been nearby and able to get the bullet removed quickly from Superman's chest, he would have suffered disastrous effects. Fortunately for Superman and for the rest of us, avoiding getting hit by raining gunfire, kryptonite bullets or no, can be easily accomplished. You just need to keep a level head and follow some simple steps to get quickly out of the path of speeding bullets.

If you're the target

Step 1: Do whatever you have to do to make yourself hard to hit.

If your assailant is directly in front of you, turn your body so that your center mass is perpendicular to the bad guy—that way, there's less of you to hit when fired upon.

 Law enforcement agents are trained to shoot for the center mass of the human body to ensure that a criminal is stopped before inflicting more harm. Additionally, they're trained to shoot at the criminal, not the threat. So the basic intent is to stop the gunman, *not* the gun.

Step 2: Run as far away as you can . . . now!

The farther you are from the shooter, the harder it will be for him to hit you. This will be especially true for an untrained assassin, whose accuracy will likely end at around 60 feet (18 m).

Step 3: Run in an irregular pattern.

It's important that you run away as fast as you can, but it's essential that you do not move in a straight line. Weave back and forth, and make it as difficult as possible for the shooter to line up a shot.

Step 4: Exit the field of fire.

Your shooter may not be a crack shot, but if he has a rifle or assault weapon, he can aim or spray bullets in your direction and hope for a hit. Your best bet: Exit the field of fire by turning a corner as quickly as you can.

If you're caught in the crossfire

Step 1: Get as low as you can.

A curb can save your life. Since most shooters fire at head height—and stray bullets are likely to be a few feet off the ground—drop down and hug the pavement when the bullets start flying.

Step 2: Stay away from walls.

If you're in the street when a gun battle begins, don't seek cover by staying close to a wall. Bullets don't ricochet predictably, so you should be less concerned with so-called trick shots popularized by cowboy movies than with a bullet flattening out and traveling along a flat surface until hitting you.

Step 3: Seek cover behind large objects.

If you're close to a car, run to the side opposite the source of gunfire, and take cover by lying behind a tire.

Step 4: Stay down until the gunfire stops and the police arrive.

Superman crouches to avoid Metallo's Kryptonite bullets, which come at head height.

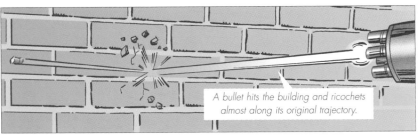

A bullet hits the building and ricochets almost along its original trajectory.

How to Block Bullets

In the movies, bulletproof vests often seem to make heroes as impervious to normal bullets as Superman. But cops or soldiers clad in Kevlar vests or ceramic body armor can only boast limited protection from gunfire. The average good guy, with just his good intentions to protect him, should consider staying indoors when the bullets fly. Even if you can track down the same protective gear used by the professionals, don't forget that it doesn't offer perfect cover. Make sure you understand the limitations of your equipment.

 Use a riot shield.

Employed by police during riot situations, ballistic riot shields are 3 to 4 feet (.9–1.2 m) in length and 20 inches (50 cm) wide and are molded from Lexan polycarbonate (bulletproof glass) in varying degrees of thickness (usually no less than 4 mm). Policemen carry these shields into riots, holding them high enough to cover their faces and torsos. The shield's dimensions make it ideal for crouching behind. Small- to average-caliber bullets will flatten out when they strike the polycarbonate surface, essentially losing penetrating power and falling away—probably the closest thing to bullets bouncing off as you're likely to get.

 Wear a Kevlar vest.

Kevlar vests, the "soft" body armor used by many law enforcement agencies, are effective in stopping mostly small arms, up to and including 9-mm weapons and .357 shots. Faster bullets, such as .223 rounds from an AK-47, will cleave Kevlar like a hot knife through butter. High-powered rifles or shotguns will also penetrate Kevlar. And interestingly, arrows, knives, and even ice picks will slice through the so-called bulletproof vest. So if you know that a bad guy is wielding only a small-caliber weapon, Kevlar will probably stop his bullets from riddling you. Otherwise, consider something tougher.

 Wear ceramic armor.

"Hard" body armor uses ceramics technology in the form of strategic arms protective inserts (SAPI). SAPI plates are ceramics composed of boron carbide or silicon carbide, chemical composites that are relatively light and can be placed strategically throughout a body-armor vest. As opposed to Kevlar, which causes small slugs to "pancake" instead of penetrating, composite ceramics are designed to diffuse impact and fall apart when struck with ballistics force. Thus, hard body armor is essentially a "one-shot" system of defense, at least where the struck plate is concerned. An impact can still be felt—grateful survivors liken the experience to being hit with a sledgehammer. While the ceramic vest prevents the bullet from penetrating, the impact can cause contusions or even heart or liver damage if the bullet strikes near those vital organs.

How to Leap in a Single Bound: Pole Vault

It's well known that Superman can leap tall buildings in a single bound (although it's often easier for him simply to fly over them). While even small buildings would be a struggle for trained athletes, there is a simple way for you to get some super-height the next time you need to get someplace higher fast: the pole vault. Mastery of the pole won't be enough to take you over a skyscraper, but you'll soar much higher than you could with just a jump.

Step 1: Choose a pole.
Most pole vaulters use a fiberglass pole 11 to 17 feet (3.3–5.2 m) in length, engineered to support approximately 165 to 220 pounds (75–100 kg). Generally speaking, the longer the pole, the higher you'll be able to jump. In an emergency, you may be forced to improvise with whatever is at hand. At the very least, be sure to choose a pole that can support your weight.

Step 2: Grip the pole.
The higher you grip the pole, the higher you'll jump. If you are right-handed, begin by gripping the pole with your right hand in the "high" position and the left hand 1 to 2 feet (30–60 cm) down the pole. Grips and hand positions vary with the vaulter. You should hold the pole so that you can plant its far end by raising both arms, right hand higher, when you're ready to vault.

Step 3: Carry the pole.
As you get ready to run, carry the pole on your right side if you are right-handed, with your right elbow bent at an angle between 70 and 90 degrees.

Step 4: Run.
With rhythmic strides, begin your run toward the pit or fixed point where you will plant the pole. The faster you run, the more momentum you'll add to the vault, thus converting horizontal energy from the run into vertical energy for the vault. The pole should remain steady. Angle it upward and away from you at the start.

Jimmy started with the pole pointing upward but is now angling it downward for the plant.

Jimmy plants the pole, gripping it close to him.

The pole bends.

Jimmy kicks off to rocket high into the air.

Jimmy thrust his legs forward and twists his body while letting go of the pole.

Jimmy lands on bent legs and prepares to roll over.

How to Leap in a Single Bound: Pole Vault   43

Step 5: Begin to lower the pole.

About midway through your run, the pole should be almost parallel to the ground.

Step 6: Plant the pole.

Gradually lower the pole as you near the plant point—whether it's a planting box or other fixed object—and hold it as close to your body as possible. Your hips and shoulders should ideally be square to the planting point at this stage. Plant the pole by driving it into the box or fixed point. Your high hand (right if you are right-handed) will grip the pole as it bends and pulls you upward. By accelerating as you plant the pole, you transfer kinetic energy from the run directly to the pole. This energy is then converted into potential energy as the pole bends under your weight and the force of planting.

Step 7: Take off.

Ride the bending pole. Kick up and grip the pole firmly to catapult you upward. The potential energy of the bending pole is thus converted back into kinetic energy as it straightens out and returns to its original shape in springlike fashion, propelling you upward.

Step 8: Thrust your legs high, and twist your body.

As you near the end of the pole's upward thrust, shoot your legs out high, and twist your body up and over the obstacle or to gain more distance.

Step 9: Let go of the pole, and push it away from you.

Step 10: Get ready to land.

Track and field pole vaulters usually have a thick pad to cushion their landing. They come down on bent legs and then roll over to minimize the impact on their knees. Remember this as you come down. To prevent injuries, you might consider tucking into a judo roll and slapping the ground to expel the kinetic energy.

 Ukrainian Sergei Nazarovich Bubka holds the highest pole vault on record, having leaped 20 feet, 2 inches (6.14 m) in 1993, nearly the height of a two-story house.

SUPER MEN: REAL-LIFE MEN OF STEEL

Superman could break world records in every athletic or competitive event. But let's give the real-life champions their due by acknowledging the feats of strength, speed, and stamina that currently top the *Guinness World Records* in human achievement as compared to Superman's celebrated superpowers.

Able to Leap Tall Buildings in a Single Bound

Cuban athlete Javier Sotomayor holds the high jump world record. He leaped 8 feet, 5 inches (2.56 m) in 1993. American Mike Powell is distinguished for leaping laterally, holding the current long jump record with a distance of 29 feet, 4.5 inches (8.95 m), recorded in 1991. And while Superman can hop over skyscrapers without breaking a sweat, Australian runner Paul Crake holds the distinction for running all 1,576 steps within New York City's Empire State Building in 9 minutes, 33 seconds in 2003—more than a single bound but certainly one for the record books.

Faster Than a Speeding Bullet

Speaking of fast—and excluding Superman and the Flash—the world's fastest man is American sprinter Tim Montgomery, who ran the 100-meter race in a record-setting 9.78 seconds in 2002.

More Powerful Than a Locomotive

In 1999, Slovakian muscleman Jurag Barbaric pulled 20 freight cars filled with scrap iron along a railway a distance of 14 feet, 9 inches (4.49 m). At 9,842 tons (8,928 metric tonnes), this feat of strength qualifies Barbaric as one of the world's strongest men.

It's a Bird, It's a Plane

The Man of Steel has flown to the farthest reaches of outer space, traveling well beyond the Milky Way galaxy on more than one occasion. But the human record holders for farthest distance traveled from Earth are *Apollo 13* astronauts Jim Lovell, Fred Haise, and Jack Swigert, who were 248,655 miles (400,000 km) from Earth when their troubled spacecraft reached apocynthion, the farthest point of their path, on April 15, 1970, as they rounded the far side of the moon in a desperate bid to return safely home.

How to Leap in a Single Bound: Long Jump

Superman doesn't really need to leap over long distances—he can simply fly, or even run extremely quickly. But for the average good guy, being able to jump over a long distance is almost a necessary skill, useful in many life-threatening situations. With the kind of alien attacks and super-villain strikes that frequently threaten to break Metropolis in two, being able to leap over a gaping chasm in downtown Metropolis could enable you to save many lives. As you'll see, the longest jumps require a running start. The key is to combine your forward momentum with a mighty leap. By following the steps below, you'll be flying through the air in no time.

Step 1: Choose your mark.

Track and field long jumpers run toward a designated line at the end of their running lane, taking care to jump before or directly from that mark but not beyond it, which would result in the jump's disqualification. Consider your mark the point where the ground gives way to nothing but air and certain doom if you step too far, giving new meaning to *disqualification*. Before you start your run, make sure that the path to your mark is clear. If you have time, remove any debris that might keep you from reaching your top speed or send you skidding over the edge.

Step 2: Begin to run.

Start out by running as fast as you can. Your goal is to attain the maximum speed possible before jumping.

Step 3: Jump when you reach the mark.

At the mark, jump outward. In addition to simply leaping feet-first as far as you can, you might consider experimenting with the two basic methods used by long jumpers to attain maximum distance (almost 30 feet [9.1 m] for many modern athletes):

The Hang Method: This involves taking off with a driving motion, your leading leg flexed and driven upward, then extended backward to join the takeoff leg so that both legs are together for landing. As you "hang" in the air, your arms will circle downward and backward, and then upward and forward. To land, thrust your legs forward with your knees flexed and bent to avoid injury as you come down.

The Hitch Kick Method: After liftoff, flex your leading leg at the thigh so that your stride continues in the air. Your legs will continue to run—hitching and kicking—as will your arms, giving you the appearance of running through the air. You can land by flexing and bending your knees, drawing them together before impact, or continuing the run and simply running through the landing— which would be ideal if you were escaping some calamity and had to put significant distance between you and it as soon as possible.

 Long jumps in the athletic arena are measured to the point where the jumper's feet hit the sand of the landing pit. If an athlete tumbles backward, the jump is measured to the distance tumbled back, not the initial landing point.

HOW TO ACHIEVE SUPER-SENSES

Thanks to the rays of Earth's yellow sun and his unique Kryptonian physiology, Superman's senses are super-acute. He can hear, smell, and see better than anyone else on the planet. Unfortunately, barring technological tricks, the average good guy cannot improve his senses on the exponential order that Superman exhibits. However, it is vital to maintain healthy hearing, sight, and smell so your senses are primed to alert you to danger.

Hearing

For persons suffering hearing loss or deafness, hearing aids or cochlear implant devices can restore hearing to limited degrees of normal. People with perfect hearing should never don hearing aids to "improve" their hearing. Essentially, a hearing aid will turn up the volume by nearly 30 decibels—amplifying all sounds to such a degree would damage your ears. For example, a running vacuum cleaner typically measures 70 to 80 decibels. The decibel "danger zone"—or point at which damage to hearing occurs—is in the range of 90 to 100 decibels. Thus, a person with normal hearing who dons a hearing aid will hear a running vacuum cleaner at 100 to 110 decibels. Some of the loudest rock concerts proudly boast loudness ranges of 120 to 135 decibels, levels that can irrevocably damage hearing by bending, shearing, or breaking the minute hair cells in a person's ear that conduct nerve impulses from the ear to the brain.

While researchers are actively seeking ways to limit or reverse this sort of damage, the proven way to avoid hearing loss is to protect yourself from extended exposure to excessively loud noises. Protective headsets should be worn during limited exposures. The recommended measure to protect your ears is to wear foam earplug inserts. Worn correctly, the foam plugs should be rolled tightly between thumb and forefinger and then gently pushed into the ear canal so that the end of the plug is flush with the opening of the canal. You should hold the plug in place as the foam expands so that it doesn't push its way out of the ear canal. If you practice preventive maintenance of hearing over time, you should be able to discern all the sounds associated with people signaling that they're in distress.

Sight

Persons suffering some forms of vision loss can have their sight restored via a variety of treatments, including corneal transplants and LASIK surgery, or external aids, including glasses and contact lenses. The human norm for visual acuity is the oft-mentioned 20/20 standard as measured on the Snellen Chart. Essentially, 20/20 refers to being able to see accurately a letter of a certain size at 20 feet (6 m). The first number is the test distance, while the second is the distance from which the average person can identify the letter. Thus, 20/20 represents 100 percent efficiency in vision. Of course, the average person cannot improve visual acuity beyond 20/20 mostly because of the amount of cones present in the retina. The more densely packed a person's cones are, the greater the ability to see long-wavelength light. People with higher densities of cones in their retinas see better as a result. Barring that genetic uniqueness, you should instead focus on protecting your vision. Consuming vitamins rich in zinc or selenium can help forestall natural retina problems with advancing age.

Avoidable physical damage to the eye is probably the greater concern. Polycarbonate lenses, such as the spectacles worn by Clark Kent to preserve his secret identity, can protect your eyes from vision-stealing injuries. Eye protection such as safety goggles or safety glasses should be worn any time small debris might be ejected into your eyes, thus scratching a lens or cornea, or worse. Ultraviolet light also poses a serious risk to vision. You know not to look directly into the sun lest you burn out your retina with focused sunlight, but indirect UV rays from relaxing on a beach or in the water can cause similar harm. That's why it's best to wear sunglasses in bright sun or don a hat with a wide brim. A telescope can replicate Superman's telescopic vision, a microscope his microscopic vision, and night-vision lenses can imitate Superman's ability to see in the dark.

Taste and Smell

The senses of taste and smell often work in tandem. Unfortunately, there is no way to become a super-taster or super-smeller. The sense of taste works when food reacts with saliva to activate the taste buds lining the surface of the tongue and parts of the throat. Gustatory nerves in the buds relay messages to the brain to identify the four basic tastes—sweet, sour, salty, and bitter—

which in combinations form flavors that are remembered in the taster's brain. Smell works when olfactory nerve cells in a person's nasal passages sample odor molecules in the air, relaying messages directly to the brain to identify (and qualify) odors both good and bad.

How well someone tastes or smells is based directly on the number and health of these gustatory and olfactory nerve cells, either of which can be damaged by various illnesses, thus reducing a person's sense of taste or smell. For example, tobacco use—either smoking or chewing—has been noted to reduce both senses. Nasal tumors or polyps can limit a person's sense of smell. Blows to the head or brain trauma may also cause a cessation of these senses. Even something as simple as burning one's tongue can degrade or remove taste buds. The good news is that both senses seem to work most acutely between the ages of 30 and 60; thus—like a good wine improving with age—a person's olfactory and gustatory refinement improves the older one gets.

Chapter 2

Super-Rescues

Superman's powers can make even the most astounding rescue look easy.

Of course, protecting the entire globe often involves super-rescues.

The following skill sets may seem impossible: worst-case scenarios requiring nothing less than superstrength and equally incredible stamina to save the day.

Quite the contrary, actually.

While bodily strength is important in swimming out to save someone drowning in a flood or riptide, superstrength is not a requirement to pull it off. An understanding of basic physics is the most important trait when rescuing someone buried under a heavy object or trapped in a teetering car. The same simple science will help you extricate someone from a quicksand deathtrap, as will a calming influence and a soothing voice.

And you'll also see, among other super-rescue skills, that X-ray vision isn't necessary to find someone buried in an avalanche; instead, keen observational skills can make the difference between life and death.

Sometimes it's just a matter of being in the right place at the right time.

And if you commit this chapter's important information to memory, you'll know the right thing to do when faced with performing these super-rescues in a variety of settings.

How to Stop a Runaway Car

Superman doesn't have much use for cars—after all, when you can fly through the skies, paying for gas seems like a very unnecessary expense. Lois Lane, however, has been known to get into her share of scrapes with automobiles. In one version of the legend of her first meeting with Superman, Lois's car plummeted off a bridge, and Superman came to her rescue. In the aftermath he generously granted the beautiful reporter an exclusive interview. He later found out she'd planned the whole thing; she'd seen him in action in his first public rescue and was eager to get a closer look, so she disabled her car, stashed an aqualung behind her seat, and took a drive near the river in Metropolis. If you're a crack reporter, sometimes you have to risk your life—or at least your car—to get the story. Lois lucked out when the Man of Steel arrived, but there are ways to stop a car with no brakes before it goes off the road.

From inside the car

Step 1: Turn on the hazard lights.
It's crucial to warn drivers on all sides that you're experiencing car trouble as quickly as possible.

Step 2: Take the car out of gear.
Take the car out of gear, whether it's an automatic or standard shift. Thus disengaged, the car's drivetrain isn't trying to propel it forward any longer.

Step 3: Head toward a hill (if possible).
Depending on where you're driving, you can steer toward a hill in the hope that the upward angle will slow your forward momentum. If the car does slow significantly, try turning off onto a level road, and then put the car in reverse, as described in step 4. However, even if you find a hill, it may have only a temporary effect.

Lois Lane's car won't brake.

She quickly takes her car out of gear.

Lois drives the car up a hill in an attempt to slow it.

Lois puts the car in reverse.

Lois takes the car out of gear again, applies the parking brake, and pulls over.

Step 4: Put the car in reverse.

Try to put the car in reverse. This will slow the vehicle as the drive tires attempt to suddenly reverse and go in the opposite direction (accompanied by the smell of burning rubber). Once the car's forward momentum has slowed drastically, drop the car out of gear again, and then turn off the engine.

Step 5: Apply the parking brake.

Thus slowed, you should be able to pull over to the side of the road and stop the car completely by applying the parking brake.

Step 6: Once the car is stopped, put the car back into gear, and secure it.

Keeping the engine off, put the car back into gear so that it doesn't roll away. Exit the vehicle, and depending on the angle of incline, wedge rocks or other heavy objects in front of or behind the tires to keep the car from rolling.

From outside the car

Step 1: Communicate with the driver (if possible).

First, try to communicate with the driver of the runaway vehicle. Tell the driver how to apply the steps above for stopping the car from inside. Remember to be patient but also clear and concise, and don't let either of you get distracted.

Step 2: Accelerate past the runaway car, and pull in front of it.

If you can't communicate with the driver because she is incapacitated, you'll have to take charge yourself, Superman-style. Since the weight and forward momentum of a speeding automobile are far more powerful than anything the average person can handle, the only real way to stop a runaway car from outside is to use another vehicle to slow the car and eventually stop it. Accelerating past the vehicle in your own car and then pulling in front of it is how to start this process.

Step 3: Slow down to match the other car's speed.

Gradually slow down to match the speed of the runaway car, closing the gap between the two vehicles. Allow your rear bumper to make contact with the runaway car's front bumper.

Step 4: Apply your brakes.

Do this gradually to slow the runaway car's forward momentum. This tactic will work best if the runaway car's gears are disengaged or if its engine is turned off. (Otherwise, you'll be trying to brake a car that is still actively trying to move forward.) If the car is off, you should be able to stop it completely by carefully braking so that neither car veers away from the bumper contact points. While braking, slowly move to the shoulder of the road if possible, signaling the driver of the runaway vehicle to carefully steer with you, if possible. Thus, both vehicles will be out of the traffic stream when successfully stopped.

Step 5: Once you've stopped, secure the car so it does not roll away.

Put the runaway car in park, and shut it off (if it's an automatic) or put it in gear without starting the engine (if it's a standard-shift). Finally, wedge a large rock or other heavy object in front of or behind a tire or tires to prevent rolling.

How to Find Someone Buried Alive in an Avalanche

Superman's X-ray vision doesn't work like your standard X-ray machine. When you go to the hospital for an X-ray, radiation is directed through your body and onto a photographic plate that records where the X-rays were stopped by the denser materials within you, such as your bones. Under the Man of Steel's X-ray gaze, nobody gets irradiated, no photographic plate is required, and he can see everything far more clearly than a doctor can by looking at a standard medical X-ray. In an avalanche, victims are often buried under almost featureless expanses of snow, and for the Man of Steel, rescuing them is simply a matter of quickly scanning the snowpack with his X-ray vision to find the victim and then digging super-fast. Luckily, there are some simple steps to follow that will help you complete your own X-ray-free search.

Step 1: Make sure the area is safe before mounting a rescue.

Avalanches occur when loose snow breaks free from a mountain's snowpack and slides downhill, traveling at speeds well in excess of 100 miles (160 km) per hour and gathering snow, ice, and other debris into an unstoppable, thundering mass. Even after an avalanche has occurred, the danger of further slides remains. Rescue attempts should be conducted in teams. Do not lead a team into an avalanche area until it is deemed relatively safe. A leader should coordinate all efforts, including posting one person whose specific duty is to watch for further signs of avalanche and give advance warning to the rescuers.

Step 2: Look for clues to the locations of avalanche victims.

Some climbers or skiers in areas prone to avalanches wear electronic beacons inside their clothing that serve as transponders for rescuers, signaling where to dig. Many victims without beacons are located based on the last location they were seen, usually buried within a cone-shaped area emanating from that spot. The point where the snow began to slide beneath the victim can signal a line of flow for a search area. Surface clues such as lost clothing or equipment (skis, climbing gear, etc.) along the line of flow will similarly provide clues to where a victim might be buried. As rescuers search, they should take special care not to contaminate the search area by dropping or discarding their own equipment, which might be mistaken for gear lost by an avalanche victim.

Step 3: Probe for possible victims.
The only way to determine if a victim is buried beneath the snow is to probe the search area at regular intervals 1 to 2 feet (30–60 cm) apart by sticking a long blunt rod into the snowpack in the hope of finding someone trapped beneath the surface. Probe in areas where a victim may have been caught, including the bases of trees and rocky escarpments. Be sure to probe piles of debris; a hapless victim could be buried beneath rocks, branches, or other detritus. Probe downhill from a designated starting point, beginning with the area in which the victim was last seen. If you find an item of clothing or other clue, mark the point and continue searching the immediate area. If you have sufficient probe rods, link each with a line of climbing cord to clearly identify the area that has already been searched. When you strike a victim beneath the snow, mark the area, and alert other rescuers to help you dig the victim out.

Step 4: Dig the victim out as quickly as possible.
While avalanches begin as the uncontrolled sliding of loose, granular particles of snow, friction will cause the resulting snowpack to thaw slightly and then refreeze, cementing in place as hard-packed snow and ice. Anyone trapped beneath the hardening surface could suffocate. When you uncover the victim, first clear the snow from around her head so that one rescuer can administer CPR (for details, see page 99) while the remaining rescuers work at freeing her body.

Step 5: Seek immediate medical attention.
Many victims are killed by traumatic injury sustained during the course of the avalanche, when they are battered and bashed by rocks and ice. Take special care in removing the victim from the snowpack, securing her head and neck in case of broken neck or other spinal injuries (for details, see page 118). Treat any lacerations by attempting to stop the bleeding (see page 103). Seek immediate medical help at the nearest hospital. Depending on how long the victim was buried, hypothermia and frostbite can threaten both life and limb.

Often the most useful (and coveted) skill Superman has is his ability to fly. But there's a lot more to flying than just up, up, and away. The Man of Steel can use his superpowers independently of one another, but his ability to fly is aided by several other powers that ensure his survival when he breaks free from the bonds of Earth's gravity.

Invulnerability

If the average person developed the power to fly, he would have to stay close to the ground for one very important reason: Within the troposphere—the zone of atmosphere extending from zero to 36,000 feet (11 km)—the average temperature drops between 2.5 and 5 degrees Fahrenheit (1–2°C) for every 1,000 feet (305 m) ascended. Hypothermia or freezing to death becomes a real concern, especially as he edges closer to the stratosphere. Most commercial jets, which are pressurized and feature heated cabins for pilots, crew, and passengers, fly at the edge of the troposphere. Moreover, all weather patterns occur within the troposphere, and a person flying through it will have to contend with lightning, pelting rain, hurricane-force winds, and other meteorological menaces.

Superman's invulnerability prevents him from feeling or being harmed by major changes in temperature or weather. In addition, when traveling at superspeed, this imperviousness to injury protects him from the adverse effects of friction, which might otherwise cause him and his clothing to incinerate.

Super-Breath

Superman's super-breath allows him to inhale or exhale vast volumes of air or other gases. He can also hold his breath almost indefinitely, a valuable ability to have when flying. Quite simply, the higher you go, the lower the concentration of oxygen, making the air thinner with increasing altitude. This isn't a problem for Superman, but mere mortals will suffer all the symptoms of oxygen deprivation the higher you climb, assuming that the drop in temperature doesn't affect you first. Headaches, nausea, and disorientation will precede unconsciousness if you don't carry some sort of personal rebreather. And if you do lose consciousness, lack of air won't kill you, but the fall just might!

Telescopic Vision

The ability to navigate successfully while flying is something the Man of Steel doesn't need to worry about. Superman's telescopic vision enables him to see at great distances—he can find a target or locate his destination by simply scanning the surface while in flight or by hovering in place. If you've ever flown in a plane, you'll realize that at a certain height, the surface of Earth appears flat. Local landmarks don't have the same definition without the perspective of standing on the ground. So how would the average good guy navigate while flying? One method would be to follow major highways or roads to your destination, but that would involve flying (or at least dropping down) low enough to read highway signs and markers, which takes valuable time away from lifesaving. With total recall, Superman has memorized maps of Earth so that he knows every route and possible shortcut. For you, a more modern tactic would be to carry a GPS (Global Positioning System) device that will display your exact location down to degrees of latitude and longitude.

How to Fend Off Wild Animals

A Man of Steel with super-hard skin has never had to worry about the bites of wild animals—at least not of the wild animals of Earth. His home planet, Krypton, had legends of some very dangerous fauna, including wolf-beasts that roamed at night in packs and giant flame dragons. In some versions of Superman's Fortress of Solitude, the Man of Steel has kept an intergalactic zoo full of strange and often deadly animals from across the stars—many of them the last of their kind, just as Superman is the Last Son of Krypton. If you find yourself taking a wrong turn in the zoo at the Fortress of Solitude and are suddenly at the mercy of the Bravado Beast, or even if you're simply worried about running into a bear at Yellowstone, here are some tips for how to survive.

Hike in large groups, and make noise.
A wild animal will usually move well away from you if it hears you coming, especially if you're part of a large group of people. As you hike, be sure to make enough noise to signal your approach to any wildlife. An animal caught unaware is always more likely to react aggressively to defend itself, its young, or its food supply. Never get between a female animal—especially a bear—and its offspring, since the animal will ferociously protect its young.

Do not feed wild animals.
Practically all national parks discourage feeding the animals living in the park. Very often, if you feed a wild animal, you're encouraging it to socialize in ways contrary to the animal's natural inclinations. An animal will expect more food, and if you don't have it, the animal may react aggressively.

Carry pepper spray or bear spray.
One nonlethal way of fending off a wild animal attack is to carry pepper spray or "bear spray" (a concentrated form of pepper spray). If attacked, simply spray the animal in the face and eyes. The animal will be temporarily blinded by the

caustic pepper compound, allowing time for you to make good your escape. If nothing else, you'll feel safer when hiking through the wilderness thus armed.

If a wild animal approaches, take a passive stance.

Back away from an approaching animal. Do not attempt to act tough or expand your chest or clothing so that you look as big as (or bigger than) the animal. Despite the belief that appearing larger will intimidate an animal, the truth is that acting aggressively may be met with even more aggression.

If attacked, don't fight back.

If a large animal, such as a Kryptonian flame dragon, attacks you, crouch down and cover your face and neck, tucking yourself into a ball. In this hunched position, you'll be better able to weather a few scratches and swipes from the animal's claws. In most cases, the animal will quickly tire of "playing" with you and depart. Take advantage of the opportunity, and get away, finding shelter as quickly as possible.

Don't climb a tree or run.

Especially when confronted by bears or other animals that are superb climbers, climbing skills will not save you. You don't want to scale a tree or other object that is easily climbed by an animal. In addition, don't run. Carnivores, especially felines, are accustomed to the chase and may follow instinctively. Bears can run at 30 miles (48 km) per hour for short distances, which is faster than you will be able to sprint even to save your life.

The Bravado Beast in the Fortress of Solitude's zoo is inflamed by the color yellow.

Lois, who is wearing a yellow jacket, backs away slowly and takes a passive stance, attempting to make herself appear as small and unthreatening as possible.

How to Fend Off Wild Animals   65

THE LEGION OF SUPER-PETS

Flame dragons aren't the only peculiar animals with a connection to Superman. Superman, like many of us, has a pet—a dog named Krypto. But Krypto isn't the only superpowered animal who's crossed paths with the Man of Steel. There once was a whole Legion of Super-Pets dedicated to serving humankind.

Krypto the Super-Dog

Superman's Super-Dog also hails from Krypton, and in addition to having superstrength, superspeed, invulnerability, X-ray vision, and heat vision, Krypto's senses of smell and hearing go far beyond the limits of human perception and even the keen senses of normal dogs. Like Superman, he focuses on rescuing people, just as police dogs help cops track down and detain fleeing felons, guide dogs aid the blind, and rescue dogs find avalanche victims. He lives in a specially reinforced kennel in the Fortress of Solitude.

Streaky the Super-Cat

With a white lightning streak on each side of his body, the aptly named Super-Cat's powers came as a result of exposure to X-kryptonite. In a bygone reality, this feisty feline was Supergirl's pet.

Comet the Super-Horse

Once the centaur Biron of ancient Greece, this transformed Super-Horse was also a friend and companion of the Girl of Steel. In addition to having the same powers as Superman, Supergirl, Krypto, and Streaky, Comet was gifted with the ability to communicate telepathically.

Beppo the Super-Monkey

In another bygone reality, Beppo the Super-Monkey was a lab monkey on Krypton. He survived the planet's cataclysmic destruction and found his way to Earth, where he was reunited with fellow Kryptonian survivors Superman and Krypto.

How to Rescue Someone from Quicksand

As *Daily Planet* staffers, Clark Kent, Lois Lane, and Jimmy Olsen have found themselves in some perilous situations in hot spots around the globe. They've fallen into danger in Mandovia, Qumar, and especially war-torn Umec—troubled countries where Superman often finds himself rescuing people but which you might have a problem finding on a map. Clark often goes missing for extended periods of time, leaving Lois and Jimmy to fend for themselves in environments where a press pass doesn't make you anything but a target and where natural disasters are the norm. If you find yourself stuck in a similarly dangerous place, one thing to avoid is quicksand. You've seen it before: Someone blunders into quicksand and slowly sinks into the viscous mix of water and grainy soil. And all the struggling in the world won't free him. Use your own super-intellect and an understanding of physics to help the victim escape what is more a dirty trap than an actual deathtrap.

Step 1: Tell the victim not to struggle.

Quicksand is formed when a natural spring or other groundwater source wells up and prevents the cohesion of soil grains (and the formation of solid ground), creating an oversaturated, "soupy" mixture of water and earth. The specific gravity of quicksand is higher than that of the victim's body, so he'll only sink so far before achieving buoyancy. He's actually more buoyant in quicksand than he would be in water. Also, quicksand is rarely deeper than a few feet. Thus, there's no danger of drowning unless the victim falls headfirst into quicksand and is unable to right himself. Struggling will only sink the victim more firmly into the quicksand. Explain this in a calm, measured voice.

Step 2: Wait for the victim to float.

Since the quicksand is denser than his body, the victim won't sink below a certain point—probably no more than to waist level—and will float. Encourage him to relax and lie on his back, allowing his legs to float to the surface. Increasing his surface area by spreading his arms out will also aid buoyancy.

Superman tells Jimmy Olsen not to struggle.

Jimmy is still, and he is now floating.

Following Superman's advice, Jimmy slowly paddles to higher ground.

Superman pulls Jimmy free.

Step 3: Encourage the victim to paddle to firmer ground.

Once he's floating, direct him to slowly paddle to the edge of the quicksand. The quicksand's viscosity will prevent him from moving quickly, but with some effort he should be able to reach firmer ground. Slow movements will prevent him from pushing himself deeper into the quicksand.

Step 4: Pull the victim free.

Make certain that you have sure footing on dry earth, then brace yourself, and slowly pull the victim from the soupy quicksand. As you leave the area, avoid marshes, riverbanks, lakeshores, and areas prone to underground spring activity —all places ripe for the development of quicksand. You don't want to get caught twice.

How to Rescue a Drowning Victim

Superman has a better relationship with the sea than most of us. He is impervious to hypothermia, can hold his breath nearly indefinitely, and can also fly up out of the ocean and zoom off to land. His fingers don't even get wrinkly if he's been in the water too long. That doesn't mean, however, that the sea holds no dangers for him; one of the greatest threats to his relationship with Lois Lane was Lori Lemaris, a mysterious girl Clark Kent fell in love with in college. Lori seemed to be keeping a secret, which drove Clark Kent crazy. It turned out she was a mermaid, and that was why they could never be together. She and Clark did manage to remain friends, which later caused Clark's true love, Lois, to briefly consider a career as a sushi chef.

Falling in love with a mermaid is probably something you don't have to worry about, but you may find yourself having to save someone who has fallen in the water. For the average good guy, saving a drowning victim will test your strength, swimming skills, and ability to breathe life into the lifeless.

Step 1: Prepare to swim.

You should try to rescue a drowning victim only if you consider yourself a strong swimmer. If you don't (and especially if you can't swim at all), entering the water will only give the next person two people to rescue. Your only recourse if swimming is off limits is to run for help. But if you're confident in your swimming abilities, begin by quickly removing shoes and other items of clothing that could become saturated with water and weigh you down. Swimming fins or flotation devices would be a great help, but chances are you'll have to swim under your own strength.

Step 2: Locate the victim so that you can easily reach her.

Establish a target line—a fixed line between yourself and the drowning victim—so that you can swim directly to her even if she disappears from sight (possibly sinking beneath the surface of the waves).

Step 3: Designate someone on the shore as a spotter, if possible.

Having a spotter on the shore to guide you is helpful; you may become disoriented if you're swimming in choppy or very cold waters. Your spotter should also call lifeguards or other emergency responders to assist in the rescue. A backup swimmer can help in securing the victim so that you don't tire too much during the rescue and need rescuing yourself.

Step 4: Swim swiftly, and pace yourself.

Don't tire yourself; you need to be able to rescue the victim and make it back to shore. Pace your strokes and breathing. You'll need strength for the return trip.

Step 5: Retrieve the victim.

If the drowning person is unconscious, float her onto her back, and hold on with one arm around her upper torso and under her shoulder(s) to keep her head above water as you swim back to shore, paddling with one hand and kicking with your feet. Again, move quickly, but pace yourself. If the victim is panicked or struggling, you will need to calm her so that her flailing does not injure either of you. Many drowning victims are inclined to grab hold of their rescuer, inadvertently pulling them both underwater. As you near her, speak reassuringly.

Step 6: Once safely on shore, begin first aid.

The strict definition of drowning is death by asphyxia following immersion in water, but there are two types you should be aware of. "Wet drowning" refers to what happens when water is inhaled into the lungs and prevents proper breathing function. "Dry drowning" occurs when a person enters cold water and the shock causes a muscle spasm in the larynx and inhibits normal breathing. Either way, check the victim's airway by lifting her chin and tilting her head back. This allows air to enter her nose and go directly to her lungs. Once she has a clear airway, roll her onto her side. Clap her hard on the back between her shoulder blades several times to expel any aspirated water. Check for a pulse. If her breathing has stopped, you should engage in CPR (page 99) until medical help arrives. If she's breathing, wrap her in towels or blankets to warm her, especially if she is suffering from hypothermia or shock.

Saving someone from a flood or similar calamity is impressive, but imagine saving the whole world. Alone or in tandem with the Justice League of America, Superman has saved the world more times than anyone can count. But he's certainly not keeping tabs. It's just what he does. For the Man of Steel, protecting his beloved adopted world is almost second nature, and he will use every power at his disposal, even sacrificing his own life, to prevent Earth from suffering the same fate as Krypton. The following are just a few of the greatest super-rescues in Superman's heroic career.

The Crisis on Infinite Earths

Superman joined forces with virtually every super hero—and a few villains, too—to halt the Anti-Monitor's annihilating wave of antimatter from sweeping over Earth and destroying the whole of reality. Infinite Earths perished as a host of parallel universes—known collectively as the Multiverse—was reduced to one single unified universe. Before it was all over, Superman mourned the death of his cousin Supergirl, who fell in battle with the Anti-Monitor. But restarting reality made way for the Man of Steel to get a new lease on life—and several new Supergirls eventually cropped up.

Doomsday

When the indestructible monster Doomsday arrived on Earth and cut a swath of death and destruction with his every step, Superman battled the creature to a standstill after his comrades in the JLA were summarily defeated. Superman stopped Doomsday on the broken streets of Metropolis but perished (albeit briefly) in the process. Superman was mourned as Earth's greatest hero.

Reign of the Supermen

In the wake of Superman's temporary demise, four replacement Supermen—later known as Superboy, Steel, the Eradicator, and the Cyborg-Superman—appeared on the scene to take his place as Earth's champion. Of the quartet, the Cyborg-Superman was a wolf in sheep's clothing, a villain plotting Earth's subjugation alongside the alien monarch Mongul. The Cyborg-Superman aided in the utter destruction of Coast City—home of Green

Lantern—turning the smoking ruin into a giant "engine city" that would remake Earth into a new roving Warworld for Mongul to lord over. However, a risen Superman—restored to full health and vigor—joined forces with the replacement Supermen, Supergirl, and Green Lantern to thwart the machinations of Mongul and the Cyborg-Superman.

Final Night

Many galaxies fell dark as the so-called Sun-Eater consumed every star in its path, leaving cold, dead worlds in its wake. Earth's heroes, including Superman, were powerless to stop the sun from being extinguished. For his part, a weakened Man of Steel—deprived of the solar rays that fueled his superpowers—did everything possible to help keep Earth's populace from freezing to death. In the end, former Green Lantern Hal Jordan—maddened with grief and turned to villainy since the destruction of Coast City—used his near-omnipotent powers as Parallax to reignite the sun, sacrificing his own life and redeeming himself in the process.

The Imperiex War

A being older than time itself, the world-devouring Imperiex sought to erase all of existence to create a new universe in the wake of the old. Thus began the interstellar Imperiex War, with Earth at ground zero. Rallying the heroes of many worlds, Superman prevented Earth's "hollowing," although hundreds of thousands perished before the Man of Steel beat back Imperiex's planet-razing probes. To honor the war's fallen, Superman changed his S symbol's color from yellow to black for a time as a sign of mourning.

How to Rescue Someone from a Riptide

The only thing that stops Superman's X-ray vision is lead, but there are some things that are invisible even to the Man of Steel. One of them is a riptide, a very strong surface current of water flowing seaward from the shore independent of other currents. Flowing several feet per second, the riptide can drag a swimmer from shore to deep water very quickly. Superman, despite not being able to see the rip, would be able to swoop in and grab the swimmer free. But by following these steps, you, too, can save a swimmer caught in a riptide before he's washed out to deep and forbidding waters.

Step 1: Swim out to the victim.
Don't fight the current. The rip is simply too strong for the average swimmer. You'll only tire yourself out by attempting to swim against the current, which flows perpendicular to shore. Let it carry you to the victim.

Step 2: Retrieve the victim.
Float the victim onto his back, and grasp him across the upper chest. Paddle with one hand, and kick with your feet. If the victim is panicked or struggling, you will need to calm him so that his flailing does not injure either of you.

Step 3: Get out of the rip.
Typically, riptides aren't so wide that they can't be escaped by swimming several feet to the side. Before you're swept too far from shore, attempt to escape the riptide not by swimming against it but by swimming parallel to the shore.

Step 4: Swim to shore, and initiate lifesaving measures.
Once free of the riptide, swim steadily to shore, keeping the victim's head above water. If possible, signal to someone to call emergency services. Once ashore, begin CPR (see page 99) if the victim is not breathing, and wait for medical help to arrive. Wrap him in towels or blankets to warm him, especially if he is suffering from hypothermia or shock.

Jimmy struggles fruitlessly against a riptide.

Lois Lane lets the riptide carry her out to Jimmy.

Lois swims parallel to shore to get out of the riptide, dragging Jimmy with her.

How to Rescue a Flood Victim

Despite the fact that Metropolis's main and central borough, the island of New Troy, is totally surrounded by two rivers, flooding is one of the few catastrophes the city has not regularly faced. Smallville, where Superman grew up, is a different story, however, having experienced many floods over the years—floods that threatened the lives of Ma and Pa Kent. While Superman can scan turbid floodwaters with X-ray vision to find lost victims, the average good guy is often hampered by weather and the dangers inherent in raging floodwaters. To save someone from a flood, it's best to follow the rescue worker's mnemonic mantra: *reach, throw, row, go.*

Step 1: Reach.

Don't follow your initial instinct to jump into floodwaters in an attempt to swim to a victim and pull her to safety. Strong currents make navigating floodwaters precarious, and you will also have to contend with the dangers posed by heavy debris that was swept up in the flooding. Your best bet is to reach the victim from dry ground, using a pole, pike, or other long object to snag the victim as she sweeps past you.

Step 2: Throw.

If possible, throw a life preserver or other flotation device to the victim. Clutching a life vest could keep the victim buoyant until rescuers arrive. Or consider throwing a line tethered to a fixed object (such as a tree or other securely anchored item) so that the victim can grab hold of it and you can reel her in. Oftentimes, rescue workers will race ahead of a victim caught in flooding waters, quickly setting up a drag line over the water to snag the victim and prevent her from being swept away. Resist the temptation to tether yourself to a tree or other fixed object and then enter the water to attempt a rescue. Your tether could become severed or—worse still—entangled in debris that might pull you under a heavy current and cause you to drown.

Martha Kent clutches the life vest Jonathan threw her to stay afloat.

Jonathan Kent has tethered the line he's throwing to Martha to a tree, so he can reel her in.

How to Rescue a Flood Victim 79

Step 3: Row.

Rowing out in a small boat to retrieve a victim of floodwaters is also an option, but depending on how swift the water is, you might expend all your energy just trying to reach the victim. Additionally, a boat or canoe could tip over in turbulent currents, also putting you at risk for drowning. Motorized watercraft are better options for reaching the victim, mainly because they'll match or exceed the current to effect a rescue and also race against the current to return to shore if you succeed in retrieving someone.

Step 4: Go.

When all else fails, go for additional help. There is strength in numbers. Rescuers can form human chains to pull victims from floods, ensuring that each rescuer is not in turn pulled into the rushing water. Once the victim is pulled to dry land, begin lifesaving measures if she is unconscious, and seek immediate medical attention.

How to Free Someone Trapped Under Heavy Objects

You'd think that if a building collapsed in Metropolis, the people trapped beneath the fallen debris could rest easy knowing that the ever-vigilant Man of Steel would soon dig them free. But, unfortunately, building collapses are not a rare event in Metropolis, to the point that even Superman might have some problems keeping up with what often resembles a citywide Falling Building Zone. So if you come across someone trapped under a heavy object, whether an entire collapsed building or just some rubble, it might be a good idea to help out instead of waiting for Superman. Of course, Superman's Herculean strength gives him a distinct advantage, but with a little know-how (and the right tools), you can still save the day.

Lever and Fulcrum Method

Step 1: Gather your tools.

In a building collapse, you can cadge a lever and fulcrum from materials in the debris and use them to free someone trapped beneath fallen timbers or crumbling masonry. For a lever, find a sturdy length of wood or metal, such as a crossbeam or piece of rebar (a concrete reinforcing bar, common in modern construction). Broken masonry or loose beams and timbers in the debris can also be used as a fulcrum. Just be sure that the material is sound and will not break under the weight of the lever.

Step 2: Position the lever and fulcrum.

Place the fulcrum so that your lever will lift the debris just enough for her to slip free without danger of being trapped further or crushed if the load slips from the lever. With the fulcrum supporting the lever, maneuver the lever under the debris.

Step 3: Lift the debris.

Push down on the free end of the lever. The downward force you exert is magni-

A metal beam acts as a fulcrum. Jimmy has placed the lever as close to Lois as possible.

fied via the fulcrum and transferred to the other end, lifting the debris. The longer the lever, the less force you'll need to apply. Lift just enough to provide access for the victim.

Step 4: Direct the victim to crawl out from under the debris.
You might want a fellow rescuer on hand to help free the victim—depending on the nature of her injuries—while you keep the debris lifted off her.

Step 5: Evacuate immediately.
Once the victim is clear, gently lower the weight, and evacuate immediately. Since the structural integrity of the building is already compromised, you don't want to risk being trapped by further collapse.

Alternative Method: Hydraulic Jack

Your car's hydraulic jack—or a larger unit built specifically for firefighters and rescue workers to stabilize overturned vehicles—can lift debris clear of a trapped victim and is particularly useful if space is at a premium or the lever and fulcrum method isn't viable amid the scattered rubble. In a building collapse, exposed wires and broken gas lines pose additional risks. Consider buffering the jack's metal surface with scraps of clothing or wood if lifting other pieces of metal. This will help prevent metal-on-metal slippage, as well as avoid any potential sparks that might cause seeping gas to ignite and turn the collapsed building into an inferno.

Alternative Method: Manual Winch

Less practical for use in rescuing someone trapped under debris is a manual winch or "come-along," both of which are used to great effect in garages to lift cumbersome engine blocks up and out of vehicles. Because this simple machine requires a fixed anchor point above the load, it may not be practical, especially in a building collapse where a shattered roof or other fractured supports can come down at any moment.

Superman might not need a winch or a jack to lift something heavy, but that doesn't mean he never needs a little mechanical help. Batman has his utility belt and Batmobile. Wonder Woman wields a golden lasso and invisible jet. And even the Man of Steel has some special equipment to save the day. The following are just a few of the super-tools in Superman's arsenal.

Super-Rebreather

Before he increased his lung capacity and was able to hold his breath indefinitely, Superman needed a concentrated air supply to survive long periods in outer space. Professor Emil Hamilton built one such breathing apparatus for Superman (later linked to a teleportation harness provided by Vegan freedom fighters known as the Omega Men), which helped the Man of Steel traverse vast distances in the blink of an eye.

Mother Box

A gift from the New Gods of New Genesis—ancestral foes of Darkseid—this sentient mini-computer can heal most injuries, even those suffered by a Man of Steel. It summons teleportation devices called Boom Tubes, cylindrical space warps that open and close in a thunderous "Boom!" The Man of Steel used his Mother Box to battle Doomsday on Apokolips.

Containment Suit

When he was once converted into a being of pure energy—known familiarly as Superman Blue—the Man of Tomorrow needed a specialized containment suit made up of microcircuitry to prevent his energies from dissipating entirely. Ironically, LexCorp provided the advanced polymer fabric, which was adapted to Superman's special needs by Professor Hamilton.

Signal-Watch

Although worn by Superman's best friend, Jimmy Olsen, this high-tech timepiece emits a hypersonic trilling sound audible only to the superhearing of the Man of Steel. Jimmy uses the signal-watch to alert Superman to trouble in Metropolis or when Jimmy needs super-saving.

Kryptonian Warsuit

Floating within a nutrient-rich bio-solution within the oversized Warsuit's chest cavity—the pilot's "womb"—Superman has operated this relic of Krypton's many conflicts as an armored juggernaut to combat several of his most powerful enemies, including the dream-invading Dominus. It is outfitted with ion pulse cannons and super-strong armored limbs.

Supermobile

With a lead-lined fuselage to shield him from the rays of deadly kryptonite, this seldom seen but fondly remembered flying vehicle even sported a pair of telescoping steel-hard fists, which allowed Superman to deliver a one-two punch from the safety of the Supermobile's reinforced canopy.

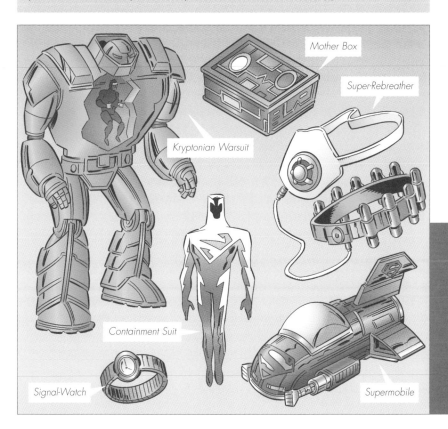

Mother Box

Super-Rebreather

Kryptonian Warsuit

Containment Suit

Signal-Watch

Supermobile

How to Save Someone in a Teetering Car

One of the most notable architectural features of Metropolis is its network of elevated highways, jutting between and sometimes through buildings. So it's not really the craziest sight in Metropolis to see a car careen out of control and wind up teetering over a cliff or the side of a bridge. Sure, the Man of Steel might swoop out of the blue sky at any second to pull the vehicle back up to safety or tote it to solid ground with the softest of landings. But since you never know when Superman will appear, you should probably be prepared to jump in and help out in the meantime.

Step 1: Find a tether.

Before extricating the driver or other potential victims, you need to shore up the unstable vehicle so that it won't fall further and is thus relatively safe for rescue measures. The first step is to find a cable, chain, or heavy rope strong enough to be used as a tether to briefly support the weight of the teetering vehicle.

Step 2: Attach the tether to a secure item.

Tie, bind, or wrap the tether to a fixed, secure item, such as a heavier vehicle or a telephone pole. Fire trucks have front-mounted cables and winches for just this purpose, allowing firefighters to attach tethers to wrecked cars on unstable ground. The great weight of the fire truck keeps the vehicles from sliding or falling away.

Step 3: Attach the tether to the teetering car.

Carefully attach the opposite end of the tether to the teetering car, taking care not to apply additional weight or stress that could cause the vehicle to slip. Don't trust a bumper or the outer shell of the vehicle as tether points. Most modern bumpers are made of plastic and are designed to absorb impacts from other vehicles, not to bear the weight of the car itself. The same goes for the outer shells of most vehicles, which are often built from lighter metals than the heavier frame. Ninety percent of a car's weight is in the frame, to which all other structural parts of the vehicle are attached. Tether here or onto the undercarriage; both are ideally suited to bear the hanging weight of the vehicle until help arrives.

Step 4: Free the victim(s).

Once the teetering car is secure, free the driver (and passengers, if any). Unless rescue workers are delayed or unavailable, this is best left to professionals who can use hand or hydraulic tools to cut open a crashed car and free anyone trapped inside. Firefighters know where to cut to avoid fuel lines, gas tanks, or other dangerous areas. Depending on the level of incline, support harnesses might need to be worn by the victim(s) as they move from the formerly teetering vehicle to more secure footing.

How to Save Someone Hanging from the Ledge of a Building

Many of the same lifesaving principles you can use to save someone from a teetering car apply to a victim who finds himself hanging off a high ledge. Firefighters employ various tools to help someone off a ledge, and you can improvise your own. If you find someone hanging from a ledge or out a window, you should follow these steps to save his life.

Step 1: Secure the victim.
As with a teetering car, your first task should be to secure the victim so that he doesn't fall further. Find a rope or other strong cord, and tie off one end on a fixed object that won't break loose. Then tie the opposite end in a loop and lower it to the victim. Instruct him to slip it underneath his shoulders. If you can't find rope or other strong cord, consider using your belt, notched in one of its holes or tied off.

Step 2: Grasp the rope, and brace yourself.
Keep yourself upright and braced, with your spine straight and leaning slightly back. *Don't* lean out. If you lean your body out over the victim, you might lose the leverage you need to keep him from falling. Also, keep your knees bent slightly, using your own body as a counterweight so that the victim doesn't slip.

Step 3: Call for help.
Balanced as you are, you won't have sufficient leverage to reel the victim in. The victim could try climbing up, but one false step or missed clutch, and he could pull you both to your doom. Better to seek help from someone else to pull the victim off the ledge, or wait for help to arrive. In securing the victim, you're essentially buying him time until trained rescuers with the right equipment can make sure he's brought off the ledge intact.

Lois Lane loops rope around Jimmy Olsen's shoulders.

How to Save Someone Hanging from the Ledge of a Building   89

Lois uses her body as a counterweight to secure Jimmy.

Still securing Jimmy, Lois calls for Superman's help.

How to Enter a Burning Building

A micron-thin force field energized by Earth's yellow sun surrounds Superman's body, making him practically invulnerable—with only a few rare exceptions. Spotting a building on fire from mid-flight, the Man of Steel can rush into and out of the blaze at superspeed, making sure that not a single hair on a potential victim is singed. Superman barely feels the heat and has no fear of smoke inhalation, the primary concern for the average good guy who's entering a burning building. Obviously, the best approach is to wait for trained firefighters with the proper equipment to enter a blaze. But if rescue personnel are delayed and you have no other recourse, enter with great care, keeping the following tips in mind.

 Remember that cotton burns, blends melt.
You're better off entering a burning building wearing clothing made from natural fibers (cotton, wool, etc.) than polyesters or blends produced from petroleum or plastic by-products. The reason is simple: natural fibers burn, blends melt. Thus, natural clothing will burn off you rather than melting; blends will stick to you, causing even worse burns by adhering to your flesh rather than falling away from it.

 Cover yourself as much as possible.
It's better to enter a burning building wearing long sleeves, or even a hooded sweatshirt, since more clothing will help to shield your flesh from heat and flames.

 Remember that smoke is more dangerous than fire.
In most building fires, smoke kills more victims than fire. The majority of fires are typified by thick, heavy smoke of various dark colors (depending on what's burning), often obscuring the flames themselves. Deadly carbon monoxide is produced by all flames, as is a small amount of carbon dioxide. Another deadly gas is hydrogen cyanide, which is released when plastics and certain textiles (nylon, silk, and wool) are burned. Furthermore, fires reduce the air's normal oxygen

level as the flames consume oxygen atoms. Usually, the air contains 21 percent oxygen, but fires can bring that level down quickly, especially in enclosed spaces. Motor coordination skills begin to be impaired when the oxygen level falls below 17 percent, and death can occur below 10 percent.

Don't douse yourself with water.

Dousing your hair or clothes with water—or donning a wet towel over your head and shoulders—to keep cool in a burning building is potentially good advice, except for the fact that time *isn't* on your side. The minutes you spend finding water and dousing could be better spent entering the building to help any victims or by dousing the fire itself with water.

Stay low on entering.

It's simple physics: hot air rises, cool air remains closer to the ground. In a fire, hot, smoke-filled air will rise and fill a room from the ceiling down, leaving the breathable air near the floor. Crouch or crawl to move forward.

Steer clear of toxic fumes.

Building fires don't just produce wood smoke. Many household objects become quite toxic when burned, releasing caustic chemicals. For example, the foam filling used as upholstery in couches or other furniture produces poisonous gas that can knock out and even kill rescuers without oxygen gear. Most firefighters who've survived such experiences liken inhaling such gases to getting kicked in the chest with an anvil. So be sure to stay low and avoid inhaling any smoke or fumes.

Get in and get out as quickly as possible.

Secure the victim and make your escape. Without a breathing apparatus, the traditional "fireman's carry" of hoisting someone onto your back isn't an option. Go out as you went in, keeping low and dragging the victim behind so that neither of you inhales deadly smoke.

SUPER-INSPIRATIONS

Superman can't rush into every burning building across the world at any moment; even his superspeed isn't up to that. Luckily, there are heroes specially trained for just that kind of rescue: firefighters. As he would be the first to attest, Superman could not and would not be the hero he is today without the inspiration of countless others whose acts of leadership, discovery, and sacrifice have been the model for every good deed the Man of Steel has done. The following are merely a few great men from across the globe and throughout history whose great works Superman continues to reflect upon as he strives to be the best Man of Steel he can be.

Dr. Jonas Salk

Salk's exhaustive and often frustrating search for a method of vaccination against the flu instead led to his discovery of a vaccine for polio. The Salk vaccine has since saved millions worldwide from the crippling and sometimes fatal disease. Salk later founded the Salk Institute for Biological Studies, a think tank seeking cures for many other medical scourges afflicting humanity, including HIV and various forms of cancer.

Mahatma Gandhi

Eschewing a career in law to become a figurehead for peaceful civil disobedience and noncooperation, Gandhi first protested the apartheid class system in South Africa before returning to his native India and helping to secure his nation's independence from British rule. Despite many beatings and imprisonments, Gandhi remained steadfast in his belief that passive resistance could accomplish more than violence to engineer social change.

Teddy Roosevelt

At age 43, Theodore Roosevelt became the youngest president of the United States (1901–1909). Known famously for having said "Speak softly and carry a big stick," the Spanish-American War hero—sickly as a child but refusing to lead a sedentary life, improving his strength and stamina through exercise—guided the United States to become a more active player in world politics. Roosevelt won the Nobel Peace Prize for mediating the Russo-Japanese War and is perhaps best known for his contributions to American conservation, setting aside millions of acres of land for public use as the great national parks throughout the United States.

Simon Wiesenthal

Holocaust survivor Wiesenthal lost 89 members of his family during the Nazis' genocidal campaign against the Jews during World War II. Following the war, Wiesenthal helped to assemble evidence of Nazi crimes against humanity. Wiesenthal also doggedly pursued the capture of SS officer Adolf Eichmann, implementer of the so-called Final Solution, as well as nine other Nazi officers. Even as he approached his centennial birthday, Wiesenthal sought out German war criminals complicit in the Holocaust.

Sir Ernest Shackleton

When his ship, the *Endurance*, was crushed by pack ice during his fourth Antarctic expedition, in 1914, Sir Ernest led his entire crew safely across the terrifying waters of the Weddell Sea in a single lifeboat. During the yearlong journey, the men quite literally endured freezing cold, exposure, and starvation—but all were rescued. Shackleton's great leadership gave his men hope in the face of hopelessness, a faith ultimately paid back in full.

Socrates

One of the greatest Greek philosophers of ancient times, Socrates advocated the pointed questioning of moral and political issues of his time. The Socratic method of thinking involves asking questions of individuals not for their own edification but so that they would discover the answers themselves. Arrested for corrupting the youth of Athens, Socrates chose suicide rather than to flee the city and undermine his own teachings.

Martin Luther King Jr.

The late civil rights leader, assassinated in 1968, was the youngest man to receive the Nobel Peace Prize, awarded at age 35. A Baptist pastor and scholar, King led peaceful protests and marches that helped to end the segregation of African-Americans in America and to achieve equal rights for all. King's oft-quoted "I Have a Dream" speech, delivered to a quarter-million marchers in Washington, D.C., is remembered as the galvanizing moment of the civil rights movement in American history.

How to Save Someone Who Has Fallen Down a Well

Unfortunately, there are some skills that even the most heroically minded and well-trained good guy can't pull off without the powers of Superman. On his own, the average good guy most likely will not be able to use X-ray vision to locate someone who has fallen down a well, or completely extricate a victim from such a predicament. However, you're not completely powerless in such a situation. The following are several ways to help prolong the life of someone trapped under such circumstances until trained help arrives.

Step 1: Keep people back.
Whether the hole is a dried-up well, a working well, a sinkhole, or other confined space, keep onlookers back from the edge to prevent anyone else from also falling in. But just as important as keeping others safe, you're preventing dirt or debris from collapsing under the weight of bystanders, potentially injuring the trapped person or—worse yet—burying her alive.

Step 2: Don't climb down the hole.
Scurrying down after the victim will only exacerbate the situation. You risk collapse of the hole, and you also may find yourself trapped. With your body wedged above (or atop) the victim, you risk cutting off her oxygen and potentially suffocating her.

Step 3: Secure a tether.
If you have a rope or harness handy, tie one end to a sturdy support, such as a large tree.

Step 4: Lower the free end of the rope or harness to the victim.
If she is conscious, the victim might be able to loop the rope or harness under her hips or around her midsection. There is a risk of strangulation if secured between armpit and neck. Your goal is to keep the victim from falling further into the void.

Step 5: Attempt to pull the victim out, if possible.

Only try to lift her out of the hole if she isn't wedged into the space; otherwise, any attempt to pull her up might cause injury. The rope or harness securing the victim should pull on the victim's torso, not her extremities. Be sure that you are on stable ground so that you do not fall in yourself. If pulling her up and out isn't possible, keep her steady, and wait for help to dig her free.

Step 6: Lower a breathing tube if you have one.

Fresh air or pure oxygen is crucial for the victim's survival. If she is wedged into a tight crevasse, pressure from the surrounding earth on her diaphragm may prohibit normal breathing, essentially suffocating her slowly. Rescue teams usually carry long extensions for air bottles and can lower breathing apparatuses to a victim trapped below ground—just one more life-preserving measure until it is safe to free her.

Step 7: Wait for specially trained rescue teams.

If the danger of collapse is too great, rescuers may dig a parallel hole several feet away through which to descend to the depth of the trapped victim and then dig across to free her. As the rescuers dig, they'll shore up their rescue tunnel to prevent it from collapsing. Another tactic is to dig a lateral tunnel from several feet away, such as a nearby hillside.

Chapter 3

Saving the Day

Superman never went to medical school.

However, the Man of Steel is perhaps the most well-read hero on the planet. With an amazing memory and nearly total recall, Superman knows just what to do when treating a variety of medical disorders at the scene of an accident. Like all good rescuers, the Man of Steel will defer to trained medical personnel when assisting an injured person. But he also knows that certain injuries require immediate on-site treatment to keep a victim alive or to help reduce the severity of pain and suffering.

The following skill sets involve injuries that could happen to anyone, anywhere, and at any time. While some involve scenarios that are infrequent—including radiation exposure and electrocution—others are common, everyday calamities.

You don't need super-memory to remember the simple steps of CPR. And treating a broken limb is often more a matter of ingenuity with makeshift first-aid materials than knowing a tibia from a fibula. A few skills, including helping someone who is experiencing a panic attack or preventing a person from committing suicide, often require a rescuer to simply listen and lend a sympathetic ear rather than have academic acumen in human psychology.

With all of these skills, the most basic tenet to remember is to keep a victim alive until you can get medical treatment. After all, if that's all that Superman himself would do, you can't be expected by anyone to do more.

As you learn the next set of skills, think of yourself as performing "super-triage" in assessing an injury, applying life-preserving measures as necessary, and keeping a victim safe and comfortable until better-suited medical personnel can use the extra time you've given them to save life and limb.

How to Perform CPR

Superman is well known for lifesaving feats that are a little outside the standard person's bag of tricks. He has spun his body around at superspeed to drill into the ground and free people trapped there. He has flown into crevices in the earth to pull tectonic plates together and prevent earthquakes. He has taken hold of ailing aircraft to keep them from falling out of the sky. No one can expect you to perform similar feats in emergency situations, but there is one lifesaving measure Superman has used on more than one occasion that *anyone* can practice. With or without super-breath, everyone should know how to perform CPR (cardiopulmonary resuscitation) on a person who has stopped breathing. Even Superman's powers don't give him an advantage here.

Step 1: Make sure you're in a safe location, and call emergency services.
All your attempts at resuscitation will be in vain if burning walls are collapsing on you. Carry or drag the victim to a safe location where you can perform lifesaving measures uninterrupted. In addition, have someone call and alert emergency services. While CPR can prevent death, a victim's injuries will still require speedy attention from professionals with greater medical skills than yours.

Step 2: Check breathing and pulse.
Position the victim on his back without putting pressure on his head or neck (so as not to exacerbate possible spinal injuries), and check his breathing. If you cannot feel exhalations or see the victim's chest rise and fall, chances are he's not breathing. Examine his airway to make certain there's no blockage. If the airway is clear and the victim is still not breathing, feel the veins of his wrist or neck for a pulse. You don't need super-senses to be able to feel the blood pumping. If there's no pulse, perform CPR to attempt to restart the victim's stalled breathing and circulatory systems.

Step 3: Open his airway.
To begin CPR, tip the victim's head back, and hold his chin up and away from his neck to open the airway.

Step 4: Deliver two rescue breaths.

While holding the victim's head, pinch his nostrils shut, and breathe into his mouth. Deliver two slow and long breaths. Keep a close seal between your mouth and the victim's to ensure that your breaths do their job in inflating the victim's lungs.

Step 5: Check breathing and pulse again.

Place your face close to the victim's face. Can you hear breathing? Does his chest rise or fall? Can you detect a pulse? If the initial rescue breaths don't elicit a response, you'll need to perform chest compressions.

Step 6: Perform chest compressions.

Locate the victim's sternum, and measure two finger widths from the bottom of the sternum toward the victim's head. This is the spot where you'll perform chest compressions. Interlace your fingers, and lock your elbows, then use your body weight to compress the victim's chest 1.5 to 2 inches (3.8–5 cm) in depth. Compress 15 times over a 10-second duration, being careful not to push too hard, which can break the victim's ribs.

Step 7: Deliver two more rescue breaths.

Following the first cycle of chest compressions, deliver two more slow and long rescue breaths, and check again for breathing or pulse. If there is no sign of either, you should continue the entire cycle of compressions (15 per 10-second duration) and rescue breaths (two per duration) until the victim has started to breathe on his own or medical help reaches you. If you've completed four complete cycles without signs of life, the victim may require use of a cardiac defibrillator or other measures to jumpstart his arrested heart.

Superman tips Jimmy Olsen's head back and holds his chin up.

Superman delivers two slow and long breaths into Jimmy's mouth.

How to Perform CPR 101

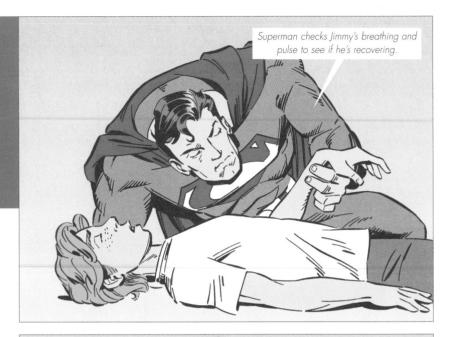

Superman checks Jimmy's breathing and pulse to see if he's recovering.

Superman compresses Jimmy's chest by 1.5 to 2 inches (3.8–5 cm), pressing down on Jimmy's sternum.

How to Treat a Cut

While he's not quite up to inventing his own new brand of laser eye surgery, Superman has been known to cauterize especially scary wounds with a controlled blast of his heat vision. But his name is Superman and not Superdoctor for a reason: Closing the wound is just one consideration when treating cuts or lacerations. Here are some steps to follow if you find yourself treating someone who's bleeding.

Step 1: Clean the wound.
Most hospitals use an antiseptic microbicide called Betadine (povidine-iodine) for cleansing cuts and lacerations. Emergency rooms irrigate wounds with sterile saline solutions. However, plain water (either bottled or from the tap) will serve your purposes by washing dirt and debris from a cut, thus minimizing the risk of infection. It's best if the water has some pressure. Squeeze a bottle of water to make it gush, or pierce a plastic bottle with a needle or other implement to create a jet spray when the bottle is squeezed.

Step 2: Control the bleeding.
Apply direct pressure to the wound. You can press a bandage right on top of the laceration. If the bandage soaks through with blood, simply apply another atop the first. If the second bandage soaks through, use another. Avoid the temptation to check if the bleeding has slowed or stopped by lifting the bandages. If the bandages continue to soak through, consider:

- Elevating the injured limb to reduce blood flow.

- Applying pressure to points in the brachial arteries to slow bleeding in an injured arm. Pressure to the femoral arteries can slow bleeding in a leg laceration. You can locate a brachial artery in the upper arm at the side closest to the chest. Look where the tricep and bicep muscles meet, and apply pressure to the pulse point there. For the femoral arteries of the legs, apply pressure at mid-inner thigh to slow bleeding below the pressure point.

- Using a tourniquet—but only as a last resort. Typically, tourniquets—bits of cloth twisted tight to cut off blood flow—are left on too long, causing ischemic or dead tissue in the affected limb. Gangrene is the inevitable consequence. Tourniquets should be loosened every 20 minutes so that the affected tissue receives some blood but doesn't bleed out anew.

- Taking care not to apply pressure to the skull of a person with a head wound. You could push bone fragments into the brain and cause irreparable harm. The best tactic is to put your hand over the occlusion to slow the bleeding until help arrives.

Step 3: Seek immediate medical help.
Take the victim to the nearest hospital. Even with your water wash, a serious cut or laceration should be treated with antiseptics and antibiotics and then sewn or stapled shut by a skilled doctor.

 When treating any bleeding wound, surgical or rubber gloves should be worn to prevent the transmission of HIV or hepatitis B.

THE ULTIMATE FIRST-AID KIT

Superman's special powers and superspeed enable him to travel light—but to be the ultimate good guy, you should probably arrive more prepared. The following list contains items you should consider when stocking the ultimate first-aid kit for responding to almost any medical situation, whether you're at home or on the road. Even the Man of Steel might find these items useful.

Durable Case
The kit should be lightweight and waterproof, featuring compartments that prevent the items in them from breaking.

Checklist
Tape an inventory of the items contained in the first-aid kit—especially medicines that have expiration dates, which should be thrown out or replenished regularly—to the inside of the lid.

First-Aid Book
A primer on first aid should be read beforehand, but keeping one in the kit can offer reminders for specific first-aid procedures. *The American Red Cross First Aid and Safety Handbook* is a great, universal first-aid resource and is available for purchase at many booksellers. It weighs a mere 1.3 pounds (.6 kg), ideal for compact kits.

Lists of Medical Resources
Include a list of important phone numbers, including poison control centers, hospitals, and other lifesaving organizations.

Medical Histories
Maintain a document of your medical history (allergies, surgeries, blood type, medications taken) in the event you're unconscious and being treated by someone else. It should also cover family members and anyone close to you. Also include phone numbers for personal physicians.

Airway Devices
Pocket face masks for CPR, oral airways to keep an unconscious victim's mouth open, and laryngeal mask airways are all crucial.

Disposable Medical Gloves
Keep several pairs on hand to protect yourself from contact with bodily fluids.

Stifneck® Collar
In the absence of this commercially available cervical collar, keep several towels of various sizes to use as makeshift cervical collars or splints. When rolled tightly, these can be used to treat neck or cervical spinal injuries.

Duct Tape
To secure makeshift splints or cervical collars in place, duct tape provides a strong and flexible adhesive.

Bandages and Related Accoutrements
Keep several shapes and sizes in your kit, including small commercially available bandages for covering minor cuts, scrapes, and abrasions; butterfly closures for deep lacerations; gauze pads for larger cuts and scrapes; gauze rolls for wrapping gauze pads and for use as makeshift slings; triangular bandages for slings or to tie splints in place; elastic wraps or splints to isolate sprains; vinyl medical tape and safety pins to secure gauze bandages; eye patches with plastic coverings for eye injuries; and skin adhesive.

Cleaning Materials
Include various items for cleaning wounds, including cotton swabs, alcohol, antiseptic wipes, sterile water or saline solutions with 20- to 60-cc syringes for irrigating wounds, and antibacterial ointments/creams.

Metal Medical Tools
Small medical tools you might find invaluable include trauma scissors with blunted tops for cutting bandages or a victim's clothing; tweezers for plucking out splinters, ticks, or insect stingers; and a number 11 blade scalpel, useful for removing dirt or debriding a wound and draining abscesses.

Mylar Blanket
This first-aid item is particularly useful in keeping victims suffering shock or hypothermia warm until help arrives.

Thermometers

A standard thermometer—preferably digital—for measuring fevers, in addition to a hypothermia thermometer to register extremely lowered body temperatures, should be stocked in your first-aid kit.

Cold Packs

These instant-activating and disposable packs can be used in the absence of ice to reduce swelling from strains or other injuries.

Sunburn Treatment

Sunscreen with SPF 15 or higher is recommended to avoid sunburn; soothing gels and other sunburn ointments should be on hand to treat serious sun exposure.

Insect Repellent

Commercial bug sprays are ideal for keeping the usual insect suspects away, including fleas, ticks, mosquitoes, and other disease-carrying pests.

Bottled Water

A clean supply of water is necessary primarily for staving off dehydration but is also useful in cleaning and irrigating wounds. In the absence of bottled water, carry a portable water purifier or water-purifying tablets.

Various Medicines

Useful medications include aspirin, acetaminophen, or ibuprofen for relief of pain and fever; antihistamines, EpiPen (auto-epinephrine injector), or prednisone tablets for allergies or allergic reactions; antinausea or motion sickness medication; topical sting medication for bee and other insect stings; antacids for upset stomachs; antidiarrheal medicines; oral glucose for treating low blood sugar; and hydrocortisone cream or calamine lotion for treating itchy rashes or insect bites.

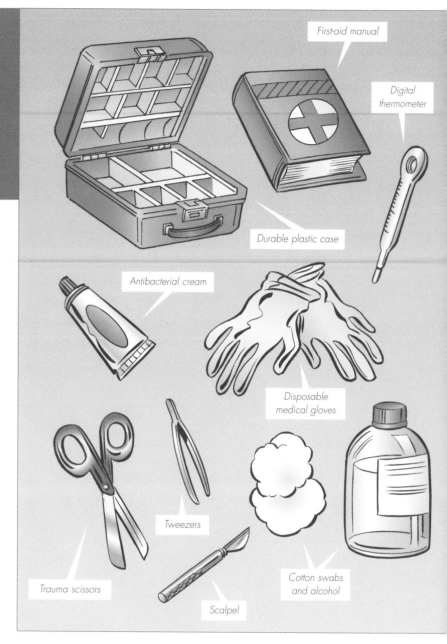

First-aid manual

Digital thermometer

Durable plastic case

Antibacterial cream

Disposable medical gloves

Tweezers

Trauma scissors

Scalpel

Cotton swabs and alcohol

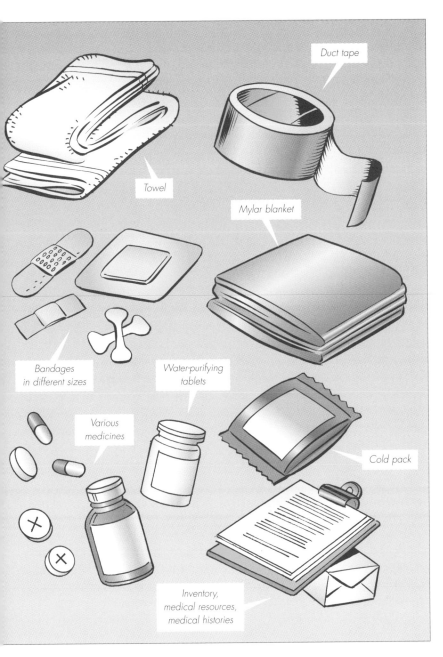

Duct tape

Towel

Mylar blanket

Bandages
in different sizes

Water-purifying
tablets

Various
medicines

Cold pack

Inventory,
medical resources,
medical histories

How to Treat an Animal Bite

Before putting on the cape and tights as Superman, Clark Kent would take time out to go to the African savannah to wrestle with lions. Not every kid trying to find himself gets to go one-on-one with the king of the jungle. And not every lion gets a fully interactive playmate who's stronger than the most toothproof chew toys. Being impervious to bites of any kind, Superman wasn't in danger, but animal bites for average guys are serious matters. Treating a cut or laceration quickly is crucial to survival, and methods differ depending on the animal that did the biting.

Technique 1: Cat bites.

Cat bites are the most worrisome, followed by human and dog bites. Cat bites can be nasty, especially when you consider the needlelike teeth of most domesticated felines. Moreover, cat bites typically transmit *Pasteurella*, a virulent bacteria present in the mouths of cats. Bites should be treated by first cleaning the wound, then controlling the bleeding, followed by a course of antibiotics to prevent infection, a risk with cat bites. Closing the wound with stitches isn't recommended, because sealing up the flesh increases the chances of an infection festering. Better to use a breathable bandage, changed regularly. There is a risk of rabies, so the animal should be watched (if possible) for behavioral changes indicative of rabies infection within 10 days of the bite. If the animal is fine, the victim won't need to suffer through rabies prophylaxis vaccination.

Technique 2: Human bites.

Staphylococcus bacteria live naturally on human skin, becoming staph infections only when allowed to enter a cut or laceration, or through a human bite wound. Human bites also transmit *Eikenella corrodens* bacteria, a natural oral flora that will subsequently cause fever, swelling, pus, and other symptoms if left to fester. As with cat bites, human bites should be treated by cleaning, controlling bleeding, and administering antibiotics after the wound is bandaged.

Punching Superman in the mouth will definitely shatter the bones from your knuckles to your elbow. But if you punch a normal person in the mouth, you may as well head straight to your local emergency room and tell the attending physician to treat you for a human bite, since you'll likely break skin on his teeth. So what begins as a right cross could end as a bite, requiring antibiotics and a nice ice pack to dull the pain!

Technique 3: Dog bites.

Dog bites don't become infected as frequently as cat bites or human bites. However, dog bites tear the flesh more often, leaving gaping wounds. Irrigate and clean the wound, control the bleeding, bandage accordingly, then follow with a course of antibiotics. As with a cat bite, there is a risk of rabies, so the animal should be watched (if possible) for behavioral changes as mentioned previously.

Technique 4: Wild animal bites.

Large carnivores (such as lions) will most likely eat you rather than leave after just one bite. A more realistic risk to most people is a bite from smaller wild animals such as raccoons or other rodents, all of which are possibly infected with rabies. The days when the offending animal would be destroyed without confirmation of a rabies infection are over. For wild animal bites, administering the rabies vaccine to the bite victim after cleaning the wound and controlling bleeding is standard procedure. With any wild animal bite, tetanus is a concern, and thus the victim should receive a tetanus booster if vaccinations are not current.

How to Treat a Burn

Should you find yourself ministering a burn victim, it's best to focus on getting the victim to a hospital. Even Superman knows full well that though his powers can save victims from fires, treating them for burns is best left to medical experts. Superman is no stranger to the direness of burns. One of Superman's greatest enemies, Darkseid, rules over a hellish world called Apokolips, where the only illumination comes from giant fire pits. A population of workers comes dangerously close to the fire pits, as they must regularly feed metal scrap into the infernos to keep the planet running. But both the Man of Steel and an average good guy such as yourself can help to reduce the pain of a burn as you transport a victim to immediate medical help.

Step 1: Stop the burning process.

The severity of a burn can be lessened by stopping the burning process. Put out the fire searing a victim's skin. Or (grounding yourself first) get him away from the live wire electrocuting him. Or pull him from the fire pit, being careful not to fall in yourself. Once the burning has stopped, you can set about treating the burn itself. Dousing with water or patting the fire out is best. Fire extinguishers contain chemicals that may cause allergic reactions. Removing smoldering clothing, in the absence of extinguishing agents, is the best way to get the burning material away from the victim's skin.

Step 2: Apply a moist dressing to the burn.

Don't put butter, cold water, or ice on the burn. Despite rumors to the contrary, butter has no proven curative effect in healing a burn. Profoundly cold substances risk causing hypothermia in the affected area, since burned skin is no longer able to retain fluid or regulate the body's temperature. Ice, while offering some temporary numbing relief, can freeze to burned skin and tear it off when withdrawn, causing even greater damage and pain. Don't put anything on the burn that might adhere to the skin and cause it to peel off when removed. A dressing moistened with cool water can be applied only long enough to get the victim to a doctor, but be mindful that any wind or breezes blowing across the dressing could cause the victim to suffer a chill. Since the skin can't regulate temperature, even mildly cool temperatures can lead to hypothermia.

Step 3: Get the victim to immediate medical help.

While first-degree burns can usually be treated at home, all other burns should be examined by trained medical personnel. Antibiotics may need to be administered to a victim suffering second-degree or greater burns. Burns caused by chemical exposure may involve treatment for inhaled gases or other toxins. Accompany the victim, and explain to medical personnel how the burn occurred so that possible ancillary injuries can be treated. For example, someone burned in a house fire will likely suffer the deleterious effects of carbon monoxide inhalation. A victim caught in an explosion may suffer blast or trauma injuries (broken limbs, sprains, contusions, lacerations, etc.) in addition to burns. A driver suffering a burned face from opening an overheated radiator may seem fine initially, complaining only of the burns and possibly a sore throat, but the inhalation of superheated gas can cause major airway complications only a short time later.

KNOW THE TYPES AND SEVERITY OF BURNS

Your skin is your body's largest organ, and it serves to protect and insulate the body, regulating temperature and shielding sensitive muscles and organs beneath a constantly regenerating and self-repairing multilayered system of flesh. Burns damage or destroy skin as a result of direct or close contact with heat, caustic chemicals, radiation, or electricity. Burn types include the following.

Flame Burns: The most common type of burn injury, resulting from skin contact with open flames or fire.

Contact Burns: Burns resulting from skin contact with a heated object that is not aflame.

Flash Burns: Burns resulting from skin exposed to explosive flash fires caused by gasoline, propane, or natural gas igniting.

Chemical Burns: Burns resulting from contact with caustic chemicals, including battery acids, solvents, or poisonous gases.

Scald Burns: Burns resulting from contact with hot liquids, including boiling water, cooking oils, or hot coffee.

Electrical Burns: Burns resulting from contact with live or exposed wires, or from being struck by lightning.

Ultraviolet Burns: Burns resulting from prolonged exposure to sunlight or artificial tanning equipment.

Treatment of these burn types is based on diagnosis of severity, with burns classified according to four degrees depending on the depth and level of damage to a victim's skin.

First-Degree Burns: These burns are limited to the epidermis, the top or outermost layer of skin, and typified by pain, redness, and moistening of affected areas. Minor blistering can also occur. UV burns (sunburns) and scalds are usually only first-degree burns. Healing time for this degree of burns is usually up to 7 days.

Second-Degree Burns: These burns extend into the dermis, the layer of skin beneath the epidermis, which is usually destroyed by whatever caused the burn. Blistering is often present, as is pain of much greater intensity than in a first-degree burn. Hair follicles and sweat glands can be damaged or destroyed. Second-degree burns are moist and red and often "weep" fluid. Although they heal in up to 21 days, this type of burn can result in permanent changes in skin pigmentation at the affected area. Skin grafting may be necessary for large burns of this severity.

Third-Degree Burns: These burns destroy epidermis and dermis, extending to subcutaneous fat tissue. Rather than blistering, a third-degree burn will be marked by leathery or charred flesh, in addition to extensive swelling. Skin color on and around the burn may be brown, tan, white, or bright red. Victims suffering third-degree burns often feel no pain since nerves within the upper layers of skin are destroyed. Skin grafting is the standard treatment.

Fourth-Degree Burns: These burns are so deep that muscle, bone, or connective tissues are destroyed. This is the most serious level of injury from a burn, often necessitating amputation of affected limbs.

How to Treat a Broken Limb

Superman's X-ray vision and other skills at times make him resemble a flying emergency room. If someone with a broken limb calls out for help and the Man of Steel hears it, he can swoop down, use his X-ray vision to verify that the victim has a broken bone, fashion splints from nearby materials (using heat vision and superstrength as needed), and then fly the person to the nearest emergency room. Luckily, even the average good guy can be almost as helpful. Just keep the following first aid in mind when dealing with a broken limb.

Step 1: Splint the limb in its current position.

Splinting a broken leg or arm is a temporary measure to stabilize the injured limb. Whether you find yourself caught in the wilderness or applying first aid on a busy city street, you might need to be creative in finding materials to construct a splint. Two sticks will suffice, but rolled-up newspapers or magazines can also provide enough rigid support, as can pillows. Your goal is to immobilize the broken limb in its *present* position. Don't try to move the limb or return it to its normal alignment. You risk further injury to the broken bone and can cause the victim unnecessary pain. With the splint materials supporting either side of the broken limb, tie the splints into place with any available material. Strips of clothing are ideal. Rope will serve in a pinch, but rope can slip, while cotton or cloth will grip more firmly. Tie a square knot, which can be easily released later. Take care not to tie the knot so tightly as to cut off blood circulation to the injured limb.

Step 2: Check for a pulse.

To make sure blood flow to a broken arm or leg isn't compromised, check the victim's pulse by pressing on a fingernail or toenail, depending on which limb is injured. The nail head should become white as you force blood away from it and then pink back up quickly when you relieve the pressure; if you're unsure, compare how a nail on the victim's other hand or foot, unaffected by any injury, reacts to the same pressure. If it takes a long time to get pink again, or if the victim cannot feel his hands or feet, he may be experiencing vascular problems related to the injury itself or the tightness of splinting.

Step 3: Seek immediate medical help.

With the limb immobilized and blood pressure within normal range, seek immediate medical help. Broken limbs, while extremely painful, are usually easily treated by setting the broken bones and applying an immobilizing plaster cast until the bones knit back together naturally. Open fractures, on the other hand, can be much more serious. Sometimes erroneously referred to as *compound* or *greenstick* fractures, open fractures are broken bones that pierce the skin and are exposed to open air. In treating these types of breaks, your major concern is to first control the bleeding (see How to Treat a Cut, page 103) and then splint the limb without pushing the bones back inside the skin. The risk of infection is decreased if you simply immobilize the injury and get the victim to the nearest emergency room, where doctors can apply antibiotics and surgically treat the injury, resetting the bones and stitching up the pierced flesh.

Lois Lane grabs two rolled-up magazines to make a splint.

Lois uses the magazines to immobilize Jimmy's leg without changing its position.

Lois has torn her jacket into strips and uses them to tie the magazines in place around Jimmy's leg.

How to Treat a Broken Neck

Even Superman's skills are limited when dealing with very serious injuries. A broken neck requires the softest touch to ensure the best possible recovery. Fast flights to a hospital will only compound the injury—which means that you and the Man of Steel are on equal footing for this task. The first order of business is to completely immobilize the victim for safe and secure transport to an emergency room.

Step 1: Stabilize the head and neck.

Emergency medical technicians carry rigid cervical collars in their ambulances to stabilize the head and neck of someone whose neck may have broken. You should use whatever materials are available to brace the victim's head and neck. Rolled-up towels surrounding the head—one around the head in an upside-down U, the other draped firmly across the neck—will serve to brace the victim's head. It's best to tape the towels down, securing the U-shaped towel across the forehead and also across the victim's neck—but not constricting his throat. Do not tie the towels down, or you risk strangling the victim. Ideally, the victim's neck should not move forward, backward, or side to side but still be stabilized in such a way as not to impede normal breathing.

Step 2: Place the victim on some sort of stabilizing backboard.

With the victim's cervical spine (neck) immobilized, her thoracic spine (chest) and lumbar spine (lower back) should be equally stabilized for transport to the closest hospital. Lacking a standard backboard, you may have to fashion something from available materials (sticks, lumber, etc.) to create a rigid litter or stretcher as wide as her back. Pad the makeshift backboard with soft materials such as strips of clothing; without them, the victim might develop sores from lying immobilized for long periods. Then secure the victim to the backboard by taping her down without compromising blood circulation. Keeping her flat and upright, move quickly but carefully to the nearest medical facility without jostling her and exacerbating her broken neck.

Paralysis and other neurological effects depend on where along the spine the neck is broken. Breaks high in the neck can cause respiratory compromise, which will require you to treat breathing problems immediately after immobilizing the victim's head and neck, very likely by intubating and inserting a breathing tube.

How to Save
a Choking Victim

All the superpowers in the world won't help you if confronted with someone whose airway is obstructed by a piece of food. Even the Man of Steel has to follow the same time-tested procedure—the Heimlich maneuver—to prevent a victim from choking to death. By knowing the signs of choking and the four basic steps of the Heimlich maneuver, you could save someone's life with just a modicum of strength.

Step 1: Grasp the victim by the waist.

If a person is clutching at her throat or gesturing to her throat and becoming red or blue in the face, it's more than likely that she's choking. Get into position behind the victim, whether she is standing or sitting, and grasp her with your hands around her waist so that you're positioned correctly to apply the Heimlich maneuver. If the victim is unconscious or you cannot reach around her waist, sit astride her hips.

Slapping the victim on the back is *not* recommended. Rather than dislodging the offending bit of food, you stand the chance of pushing it farther down and lodging it more deeply. If the victim aspirates the food into her lung, she risks pulmonary infection and/or pneumonia.

Step 2: Make a fist against the victim's abdomen.

Ball one hand into a fist, and position it with the thumb pressed against the victim's abdomen. Your fist should be above her navel but below her ribcage. For the unconscious victim or a victim lying prone, use the heel of your hand in a similar position above her navel but below her ribcage.

Superman positions himself behind a choking Lois Lane.

Superman makes a fist against Lois's abdomen.

Superman thrusts upward with his fist.
Sometimes one thrust is enough to dislodge the object.

Step 3: Thrust upward with your fist.

Holding onto your fist with the opposite hand, make a quick upward thrust with your fist pressing into her abdomen. Thrust only with your fist and hand. Do not squeeze her ribcage, or you risk fracturing or breaking ribs, the broken shards of which could puncture her lung(s) if squeezed too tightly. For the unconscious victim or a victim lying prone, make an upward thrust with the heel of your hand, using your body weight for each push. Again, do not press against her ribcage. The force of your body weight could break ribs.

Step 4: Repeat.

One thrust may be enough to expel the food or object clogging her airway. More likely, you'll need to repeat the thrust several times until the morsel is forcibly expelled. Once breathing normally, the victim should seek medical attention to ensure that she's all right. If the victim is not breathing on her own, you may have to administer CPR (see How to Perform CPR, page 99) until trained medical help arrives. For the unconscious victim or a victim lying prone, repeat until the bit of food or object is expelled. This particular victim may require CPR since choking has already cut off air to the point of losing consciousness. Simply expelling the food or object may not be sufficient to start her breathing again. Begin CPR, and seek immediate medical help for her.

How to Help a Seizure Victim

Whether you're a Man of Steel or an average good guy, helping a person suffering from a seizure involves the same basic steps, all designed to keep the victim from injuring herself until the seizure subsides and you can get her to medical help.

Step 1: Be observant.

Though it may be difficult, try to recall how the seizure began, and mark its duration. Any information you can give to medical personnel regarding the seizure's onset is invaluable for treating the victim immediately afterward, as well as in the long term for ongoing and related medical concerns. For example, someone who is hypoglycemic or diabetic may suffer a seizure as a result of low blood sugar because she had not eaten for some time, and an epileptic may suffer seizures if he has not taken his medication as prescribed. Alerting medical personnel to any prescription drugs used by the victim will help to ascertain the cause of the seizure and the treatment of any medical malady causing it.

Step 2: Call for medical help.

Tell emergency paramedics everything you observed about the seizure, as well as everything you know about the victim, including allergies and medications.

Step 3: Move furniture or any other object that might injure a seizing victim.

Gripped by a seizure, a person may thrash or convulse uncontrollably. Clear an area on the floor or ground so that she doesn't bash her head or body against anything. Do not attempt to hold her still by her arms or legs—this will only risk injuring her. The best action is to take no direct action: You can't stop or control the seizure. Better to "ride it out" and let the seizure run its course. Most seizures abate in 5 to 10 minutes.

Step 4: Turn the victim to her side, if possible.

Though it can be difficult when someone is experiencing convulsions, you should turn the victim onto her side so that she doesn't swallow excessive saliva—the "foaming at the mouth" associated with some seizures—and aspirate the liquid into her lungs. A common misconception when treating a seizure victim is that you should use a "bite block" of some sort (spoon, wallet, etc.) to prevent her from biting and/or swallowing her tongue. While a convulsing person may bite down on her tongue and lacerate it to some degree, she's more likely to bite your fingers off than to sever her own tongue while clenching her teeth. A victim lacking muscle control during a seizure could also bite down on a wooden or metal spoon so hard that she breaks her own teeth, the sharp pieces of which could in turn be aspirated into her lungs. If you lay the victim on her side, her tongue cannot flip back onto the oral pharynx and compromise the airway, thus allowing her to breathe normally—albeit excitedly—until the seizure passes.

Step 5: After the seizure, keep the victim calm until help arrives.
Following a seizure, the victim will often enter into what is called a post-ictal phase, during which she may be confused, with little or no awareness of her surroundings or memory of the seizure itself. You should avoid giving any sort of medication immediately following a seizure. Vomiting during the post-ictal phase is common, risking aspiration of materials into her lungs if another seizure follows. Brief visual impairment and temporary paralysis can also occur during this period. The victim may be combative as a result of her confusion. Simply try to keep her calm, allaying her anxieties until trained medical help arrives.

How to Save Someone Who Has Been Poisoned

Superman could, if he so desired, sprinkle cyanide over his morning corn flakes, enjoy a nice steaming cup of decaffeinated arsenic, and then brush his teeth with hydrochloric acid, all with no ill effects. But he's not totally immune to poisoning. The mysterious and magical La Encantadora managed to nearly kill Superman with a poisonous kiss made up of a lethal mixture of kryptonite and nanotechnology. The poison was identified in time to save the Man of Steel's life. You too can help save someone who has swallowed poison. By getting a poisoning victim medical help as quickly as possible, you can make the difference between life and death.

Step 1: Do not help the victim vomit, and do not administer water.
Your first inclination in treating someone who has swallowed poison may be to induce vomiting to regurgitate the offending toxin or to make him drink water in an attempt to "dilute" the poison. Do not attempt either. If he falls unconscious, he could vomit and aspirate both the poison *and* the water into his lungs. There's no telling what the poison could do to lung tissue, especially if it's a caustic substance, and the risk of aspirated fluid causing pneumonia only compounds the risk to the victim's recovery.

Step 2: Take the victim to the nearest emergency room.
Get the victim to the nearest emergency room as quickly as you can. There, trained doctors will begin their supportive care by trying to prevent vomiting, often by administering intravenous antiemetics. They will also try to keep the victim as comfortable as possible for the next step.

Step 3: Give the doctors any information you can to help identify the poison.
Though many doctors are divided on the benefits versus the risks of administering activated charcoal, this is the medical standard for treating ingested poisons. Following intubation to keep the victim's airway clear, activated charcoal is pumped into the stomach and then back out after allowing the charcoal to bind to

the poison, thus removing the toxin before it is completely absorbed. However, some poisons do not bind readily to activated charcoal, calling for specific antidotes for certain poisons or overdoses. It's important to let the attending physicians know just what poison the victim ingested and in what quantity. Any information you have that can help identify the poison will be extremely helpful.

Once the victim's stomach is pumped and the activated charcoal removed, doctors will keep close watch over the victim to treat any further symptoms or side effects of the consumption.

How to Treat Radiation Exposure

Superman's foes have employed a variety of nuclear weapons in the name of evil. The Atomic Skull is basically a walking nuclear pile; his merest touch would fry a Geiger counter. Superman's greatest weakness is his famous susceptibility to the green radiation of kryptonite, which is also harmful to humans after prolonged exposure. Lex Luthor wore a kryptonite ring to fend off Superman for many months, until the radiation from it gave him a unique case of kryptonite cancer; his hand had to be amputated to save his life. Regardless of whether the victims you're trying to help have survived a traditional bomb blast or are suffering from long soaks in kryptonite-infused baths, treating radiation exposure involves the following steps.

Step 1: Determine the level of exposure.

Assessing the level of radiation exposure is important for determining the course of treatment. A Geiger counter swept over the victim's body will measure irradiation. In addition, exposure can be measured to a limited degree by swabbing the oral or nasal passages for irradiated particles that have been inhaled. Lab analysis of the swabbing would then determine the exact exposure. A lethal of dose of radiation usually requires exposures of 450 to 600 total rads, although death has been documented at just 320 rads.

 Just sleeping next to someone will expose you to 0.1 millirads of natural radiation. A chest X-ray is 12 to 17 millirads.

Step 2: Decontaminate.

More than likely, HAZ/MAT teams will already be on hand in the event of a radiation event to begin controlled decontamination processes. If not, you should initiate decontamination by having the victim remove his clothing and shower; he should wash thoroughly, shampooing his hair and cleaning his nail beds. Scrubbing is the normal course of action for any contaminant. However, extra measures should be taken in the case of radiation to prevent any wastewater from escaping and flowing into sewers by plugging the drain of the bathtub or shower. That water is now irradiated and could contaminate more people. In addition, the victim's clothing should be disposed of properly—not incinerated, which could render some radioactive material airborne in smoke and ash. Contact your local authorities to dispose of any radioactive materials properly.

Step 3: Seek immediate medical attention.

Take the irradiated person to the nearest emergency room. There, supportive care will be initiated to treat the typical symptoms of radiation exposure, which are usually associated with the gastrointestinal tract. Drugs can be administered to ameliorate nausea, vomiting, diarrhea, or abdominal cramping. Intravenous fluids can be used to stave off dehydration. Depending on the level of exposure, airway support may be necessary to avoid respiratory compromise. Thereafter, potassium iodine is the most common treatment, with 130 to 260 milligrams of the compound administered daily for several days. Potassium iodine will saturate the victim's thyroid gland, where radioactive material would otherwise concentrate, thus preventing the thyroid's destruction or dysfunction, which can be lethal. For plutonium exposure, chelating agents such as calcium DTPA or zinc DTPA can be administered to bind to the radioactive material, rendering it inert and allowing it to be excreted naturally. Radiation burns usually indicate extreme exposure but are treated just like normal burns: wash with soap and water following decontamination.

The measure of how sick the victim becomes in the time following exposure is a good indicator of the level of exposure. If his condition deteriorates quickly, chances are that he has received dangerous doses of radiation. Blood work and bone marrow suppression may be necessary to determine survivability.

A FIELD GUIDE TO KRYPTONITE

Superman's famous Achilles' heel is kryptonite, a radioactive remnant of his home planet of Krypton. Long before the peaceful civilization that Superman was born into existed, Krypton was a warlike planet. In one of its deadliest conflicts, a radioactive weapon seeped into the planet's crust. Over millennia, it spread like a green plague, eventually leading to Krypton's destruction and Superman's being sent to Earth as a child by his father, Jor-El. Many other colors of kryptonite, each with its own effects on the Man of Steel, have cropped up over the years. Some are merely rumors, and some aren't even harmful to Superman, but many of them have been put to nefarious uses by various super-villains.

Green Kryptonite
The remains of Krypton are poisonous to any surviving Kryptonians. This substance causes immediate debilitating effects, including weakness and nausea. Within a few hours of constant exposure, green kryptonite will kill Superman and his kind.

Red Kryptonite
Various versions of red kryptonite have appeared over the years, including a magical variety that rendered Superman powerless and an artificial form developed by Batman that made Superman's skin invisible and sent his powers haywire. Another variation was formed when green kryptonite passed through a crimson cosmic cloud and was transformed into a scarlet rock that caused unpredictable effects on Superman, often altering his appearance or demeanor. This variety of red K could cause his beard to grow uncontrollably or make him evil for a brief time.

Gold Kryptonite
Green or red kryptonite exposed to intense radiation becomes gold kryptonite, exposure to which will permanently rob Superman of his powers.

Blue Kryptonite
Blue kryptonite is an imperfect form of kryptonite that affects only Superman's peculiar opposite, Bizarro, and his ilk.

White Kryptonite

Green kryptonite transformed by yet another space cloud into white K will destroy any plant life in close proximity.

Jewel Kryptonite

The remains of Krypton's wondrous Jewel Mountains, jewel kryptonite can amplify a person's psychic powers—and seems especially effective when used by super-villains. The Kryptonian criminal Jax-Ur once used its powers from his prison in the Phantom Zone to telepathically torture Superman.

X-Kryptonite

X-kryptonite is an artificial form of kryptonite created to counteract the effects of kryptonite, but the experiment was not a success. It had the peculiar effect of giving superpowers to normal humans and animals and permanently turned Supergirl's feline pet into Streaky the Super-Cat.

Anti-Kryptonite

An especially peculiar form of kryptonite, anti-kryptonite comes from an anti-matter universe where an evil version of Superman, known as Ultraman, derives great power from it. In fact, his powers diminish the farther he is from anti-kryptonite.

SUPERMAN'S SUPER-WEAKNESSES

Everybody knows that kryptonite is Superman's major weakness. But exposing the Man of Steel to the green-glowing radioactive remnants of his home planet isn't the only way to render him vulnerable. Here are a few of the major chinks in his seemingly invulnerable armor.

Magic

Superman's powers are derived from the yellow sun of Earth; they have no magical component, leaving the Man of Steel open to malignant sorcery. He has no magical abilities of his own and is powerless to stop any magical attacks against him. More often than not, the Man of Steel must resort to outwitting occult opponents, such as Mr. Mxyzptlk, Satanus, or La Encantadora.

Mental Manipulation

Superman may be the most powerful man on Earth, but he has much the same self-doubt as a normal person. He also has great concern for the safety and welfare of his loved ones. Telepathically powered foes, including Dominus and Brainiac, have used these fears and anxieties on several occasions to wage psychic war on Superman, bringing his worst fears to life and plunging the Man of Steel into nightmare realities from his own subconscious.

Red Sun

Under the rays of Earth's yellow sun, Superman's abilities are at peak power. But the farther he travels away from our star, the weaker he becomes. Under a red sun, such as the star that orbited the planet Krypton, Superman is stripped completely of his powers, becoming no stronger than a normal human until he can recharge under a yellow star.

Relationships

Perhaps his greatest weakness, Superman's devotion to his friends and loved ones is enough to give him pause in the middle of a fight. If a villain wants to render the Man of Steel powerless, all he need do is hold Lois Lane or Jimmy Olsen hostage and threaten their lives. Superman won't give up, but he also won't do anything to risk the lives of those he loves. A true hero, he would sacrifice himself to save just one life.

How to Treat Starvation or Dehydration

Superman is powered not by protein bars and a steady diet of food but by Earth's yellow sun, so he is capable of going for months without eating or drinking. The average human, however, can survive only an estimated six weeks without food and up to six *days* without water. When faced with a victim suffering such extremes of hunger and thirst, the first task is to take that person to a hospital. In the interim, consider the following steps to help reduce discomfort until you can get to professional medical treatment.

Step 1: Moisten his lips.
Victims of both starvation and dehydration often can't swallow because of dry or sore throats. Begin by moistening the victim's lips before giving small sips of water. Oral hydration will aid him in swallowing small bits of food.

Step 2: Offer food and water in small amounts.
Lost potassium and other electrolyte imbalances may necessitate intravenous replenishment of fluids and nutrients. For someone suffering starvation, consider offering small bites of energy bars, candy, or other foods rich in carbohydrates or simple sugars (glucose or dextrose). Chocolates or orange juice are ideal, as are sports drinks. Allow the victim to eat at a measured pace, avoiding the temptation to "wolf down" the food. He may risk choking or vomiting. The same goes for treatment of dehydration: Don't allow the victim to drink too fast or too much. Rehydrating too quickly can result in cerebral edema, a dangerous and potentially deadly swelling of the brain.

Step 3: Seek medical help.
The small amounts of food and liquid you offer are only meant to stave off unconsciousness and death. Intravenous fluids or even high-nutrient food pumped directly into a victim's stomach may be necessary for the most extreme cases of food or liquid deprivation. Following that, regular food intake monitored by a physician and/or dietician will restore the victim to health.

DEHYDRATION

Lois Lane is suffering from dehydration.

STEP 2

Superman carefully gives Lois very small amounts of water.

As Lois recovers, Superman helps her resist the impulse to drink too much water too quickly.

How to Treat an Electrocution Victim

While Superman can easily survive a lightning strike, he's no stranger to electrocution. At one time, in fact, Superman was electricity itself. After the Man of Steel briefly lost his powers, they returned in altered form, turning him into a being of pure energy who had to wear a blue containment suit to keep from dissipating into static electricity. Known as Superman Blue, a being without X-ray vision, heat vision, or many of his old super senses, he could now teleport from place to place, phase through solid objects, and control energy better than even the most heavy-duty surge protector. Unlike Superman, average people can suffer any number of grievous injuries after being struck by lightning or making contact with high-voltage wires. Electrocution does not necessarily equal death, especially if treated in time. The following lists just what you can do to help someone who has been the victim of a severe electrical shock.

Step 1: Secure the scene.

In many incidents of severe electrical shock, rescuers can also end up unconscious or dead by rushing into an electrocution scene without making sure that it's secure. If lightning has struck someone, you should take steps to avoid being struck yourself as you quickly take the victim to cover. Don't remain in the open during a storm, and stay low to the ground as you drag the victim to safety. If a victim has been electrocuted by a fallen or exposed power line, you need to find something made of rubber, wood, or another nonconductive material to push the live line away from the victim or to pull him to safety.

Step 2: In a lightning strike, don't assume that cardiac arrest means death.

Lightning strikes sometimes involve more than one victim, thus necessitating triage to ascertain which victim is in greatest need of care. Triage for lightning strike victims is unusual because you cannot assume that a victim with no heart activity is dead—respiratory arrest may be mistaken for cardiac arrest. Performing CPR may restore breathing, which may in turn jumpstart an arrested heart. Lightning strike victims have a greater chance of survival than other victims of cardiac arrest if you can resuscitate them first before moving on to other injuries.

Step 3: Prepare to treat multiple injuries.
Lightning strikes often cause multiple injuries in addition to cardiac arrest or less severe cardiac disturbances. Once the victim is resuscitated, you may have to treat blast injuries. In both a lightning strike and contact with another source of extremely high voltage, a victim can be thrown some distance. Typical related trauma includes fractured or broken bones, cuts and lacerations, mild to severe burns (see How to Treat a Burn, page 112), and eardrum ruptures (most common with lightning strikes).

While a bolt of lightning is essentially a quick "single-shot" electrocution, touching a high-voltage wire can be a more protracted experience, since the alternating current coursing through the line can cause the victim's muscles to contract, thus making him grip the wire uncontrollably, unable to let go. Both lightning strikes and power-line electrocutions can cause rhabdomyolysis, muscle injuries in which muscle contents and waste products from muscle tissue are electrically ejected into the victim's system, raising the risk for kidney damage or failure as the victim's body works overtime to process these secretions, which are actively toxic. Treat the most serious of injuries first, and take the victim to immediate medical care.

 The rapid expansion of gases in the atmosphere surrounding the lightning bolt—and, in turn, the victim—can cause someone's tympanic membranes to rupture in what is known as barro trauma.

Step 4: Prepare for follow-up care.
Unfortunately, survivors of lightning strikes and other forms of electrocution often face serious long-term medical concerns. Seizures and other neurological disorders may develop later. Burst eardrums should be monitored to avoid long-term hearing loss. The victim should also have his vision checked regularly, since cataracts are often a complication following direct lightning strikes. Other systemic problems, including loss of or diminished muscle control, can also result from electrocution. Keep a close eye on any problems that might develop in time, and seek medical consultation to treat any lingering side effects.

THE AMAZING STORY OF SUPERMAN-RED AND SUPERMAN-BLUE

The Man of Steel briefly became Superman Blue after his solar-powered abilities were lost when an interstellar menace called the Sun-Eater literally consumed Earth's life-giving star. The sun was reignited, but attempts to recharge the power-depleted Superman left him converted into a blue-tinted being of pure energy. Luckily, Superman returned to normal, but not until after he split into two energy beings, when a "Superman Red" persona splintered off from Superman Blue. While Superman Blue was cool and rational, Superman Red was brash and hotheaded. The two were able to work it out by merging back into one being: the original Man of Steel, complete with all of his traditional powers.

The whole adventure is similar to one of the most famous, albeit "imaginary," stories that happened when a Superman from an alternate reality made a list of his unaccomplished tasks (see below) and attempted to increase his mental power a hundredfold with a brain-evolution machine. Powered by the rays of every type of kryptonite, Superman's invention succeeded in doubling his mental capacity . . . by splitting him into two identical Supermen, Superman-Red and Superman-Blue! (A different pair of crimson and blue-hued Supermen from when Superman split on Earth.) These Men of Steel were able to accomplish the following miraculous feats:

Restore Kandor to Normal Size

The shrunken bottle city of Kandor, with its millions of microbe-sized inhabitants, remains one of Superman's most vexing still-in-progress rescues. By fusing hyper-magneton meteors to form a planetary core, the blue and red Supermen were able to attract every piece of kryptonite throughout the universe to the hyper-magneton, which reversed the transformative process that converted these remnants of Krypton into deadly radioactive isotopes. Thus, a New Krypton was formed. With an enlarging ray of their own invention, Superman-Red and Superman-Blue restored the shrunken bottle city of Kandor to full-size, finally repatriating their fellow Kryptonians! In the process, the Men of Steel also accomplished the number two task on their list: finding an antidote to green kryptonite.

Wipe Out Crime and Evil

Of course, Superman means to cure criminals of evil thoughts, not destroy them utterly. The Supermen devised an antievil hypno-ray, first testing it on warrior ants to make the insects stop their natural inclinations to devour each other. The Men of Steel then set about deploying their ray via a system of satellites encircling Earth. From petty thieves to prison-incarcerated Lex Luthor, every evil thought on the planet was replaced with the will to do good deeds. The antievil hypno-ray even worked as far away as the Phantom Zone and the Fifth Dimension, reforming all the Kryptonian criminals stuck in the former limbo-like dimension, and making over that mischievous Mr. Mxyzptlk in the latter. Superman's arch-foe Luthor developed a super-serum that would cure every known disease (and even a few unknown maladies). When Superman-Red and Superman-Blue sprayed the serum all over Earth—a few drops in every body of water—the blind saw, the lame walked, and Luthor's hair even grew back!

Choose Between Lois Lane and Lana Lang

When he was a teenager in Smallville, Clark Kent's heart belonged to child-hood friend Lana Lang. In adulthood, Clark fell head over heels for Lois Lane, but he still had lingering feelings for Lana. Superman-Red and Superman-Blue realized that having two Men of Steel meant that each could marry one of the women. Rather than flip a coin, each Man of Steel molded an L out of metal girders, and the pair flew off to the Himalayas, where they waited for a lightning storm to decide. Whoever got struck first would be able to pick the love of his life. The problem is that a lightning bolt forked at the last moment to strike both! As the Supermen pondered their dilemma, Superman-Red mused that he'd marry Lois if given the chance, which was good news for Superman-Blue, who professed his true love for Lana. The happy couples married, with Superman-Red moving Lois to New Krypton, while Superman-Blue and Lana wed and remained on Earth. Each had two children and lived happily ever after.

How to Deal with a Panicking Bystander

No one can cause the kind of chaos personified by Superman's ornery enemy Mr. Mxyzptlk. This imp from the Fifth Dimension delights in using his abilities to manipulate reality, and his practical jokes often terrify those around him. Superman's heroic presence and reassuring tone are often enough to allay the fears or anxieties of the subjects of most of Mxyzptlk's pranks, but if he's not available and you find yourself having to calm down someone in the midst of a panic attack, don't panic yourself. There's a great deal you can do to calm someone down until medical help arrives and can assess the situation.

Step 1: Recognize the symptoms.

A panic attack or panic/anxiety disorder afflicts one out of every 75 people in their lifetime. More pronounced than stress or anxiety caused by day-to-day experiences, a panic attack is a behavioral illness marked by a sudden and overwhelming fear brought on without warning, often without any pinpointed cause. Healthy people can suffer panic attacks, the causes of which are actively being researched. People suffering a sudden medical disorder, such as a heart attack or cardiac arrhythmia, may suffer a panic attack at the same time, leading to confusing symptoms.

A person suffering a panic attack may experience intense fear and at least four of these symptoms within a ten-minute interval:

- Heart palpitations or rapid pulse

- Heightened perspiration

- Uncontrolled trembling

- Hyperventilation, shortness of breath, or difficulty breathing and swallowing

- Chest pain

- Nausea or stomach cramping

- Dizziness or vertigo

- Derealization (feelings of unreality)

- Depersonalization (feelings of being detached from oneself)

- Numbness or tingling

- Hot flashes or chills

- Carpal/pedal spasms (twitching of hands or feet)

Step 2: Call for medical help, and reassure the victim.
While sedatives may be necessary to calm someone suffering a panic attack, only trained and licensed physicians should administer any form of medication. Antidepressants or serotonin inhibitors have been shown to reduce the frequency of panic attacks in certain people. Call for medical help, and try to keep the victim calm until help arrives. Try to talk to the victim about his fear, assuming that he can articulate it himself. Be supportive and reassuring. By calming the victim, you can hope to ease his rapid breathing and help his other symptoms to subside until medical personnel can arrive.

Other calming techniques to reduce the symptoms of panic attack can include muscle tension/relaxation exercises, in which the victim flexes and releases the muscles in his arms and legs to reduce spasms or trembling, and breathing exercises to control hyperventilation. Breathing into a paper bag has been shown to reduce some hyperventilation, but this technique should only be done under a watchful eye to make certain the victim doesn't pass out in the process.

Step 3: Remove the victim from a situation that may precipitate another panic attack.
Extreme and real fears can trigger panic attacks. Get the affected person away from the location where panic first set in, and take him to a calmer place (or situation) where you can engage in a dialogue of reassurance as you wait for medical help.

JIMMY OLSEN'S BLUES

Superman's best friend, Jimmy Olsen, can tell you that standing in the shadow of the world's greatest hero can be tough. For one thing, it's often difficult living up to what is almost an impossible standard for moral and ethical perfection. But the reason Superman and Jimmy became pals in the first place is that Jimmy also believes strongly in the values of truth, justice, and the American way. Superman's friendship has inspired Jimmy to heroism on more than one occasion, even though Jimmy has suffered through a great deal of chaos as well, including some terrifying, but temporary, physical changes.

Elastic Lad

Jimmy's super-heroic alter ego, capable of stretching any part of his body to incredible lengths, was first made possible by a green glowing liquid brought back in a mysterious trunk Superman retrieved from space. Later, Jimmy drank an elixir created by Professor Phineas Potter to become super-pliable on demand.

Flamebird

As teen sidekick to Nightwing—another secret identity briefly taken up by the Man of Steel—Jimmy battled evil within the bottle city of Kandor, with both heroes equipped with personal jet-motor belts to guard over the shrunken metropolis in the model of Batman and Robin.

Merman

After receiving a magic ring from a mermaid, Jimmy found himself temporarily able to breathe underwater and perform super-deeds.

The Human Skyscraper/Colossus of Metropolis

Jimmy was once transformed into a giant building but was later restored to normal size by Professor Potter. Another time, Jimmy drank a serum to grow to colossal size to capture the gargantuan super-ape known as Titano.

Radioactive Boy

Jimmy briefly emitted dangerous levels of radioactivity—enough to wither plants—after touring an atomic power plant.

The Human Flame Thrower
Professor Potter developed a way to grant Jimmy the power of flaming breath.

Animal Master
Jimmy once developed the power to talk to animals telepathically.

The Human Octopus
Albeit briefly, Jimmy grew additional appendages and had six arms (plus two legs).

Wolfman Jimmy
Jimmy once became a teenage werewolf after drinking a magic potion. Another time, Jimmy turned into a wolf thanks to the magical manipulations of Mr. Mxyzptlk.

Bizarro Jimmy
Professor Potter's "normalizer ray" turned Jimmy into a Bizarro, making him Superman's worst pal!

The Human Porcupine
That Fifth Dimensional imp Mr. Mxyzptlk stuck it to Jimmy again by transforming him into a human porcupine, quills and all.

Turtle Boy
As if being Superman's best pal wasn't enough celebrity, Jimmy gained further notoriety as the costumed host of WGBS's Turtle Boy children's television show. But Jimmy also once turned into an actual giant Turtle Boy who rampaged through Metropolis. No children in Metropolis were laughing on that dark day.

Chapter 4

Saves at Home

Can you repair a burst pipe in a pinch? How about fixing a blown fuse?

The skill sets in this chapter may seem mundane, but each addresses a real-life crisis, and the average good guy must be prepared to tackle problems both large and small. Drying out a basement is not as dramatic as a rescue from a fire or the successful performance of the Heimlich maneuver, but knowing the right way to do it could make all the difference to a friend knee-deep in floodwater.

Disguised as Clark Kent, even Superman sometimes finds himself having to refill the office water cooler at the Daily Planet or helping to fix a flat tire on the streets of Metropolis.

Broken photocopier? Power outage? Why wait for help? Rise above the crowd at the office or in your neighborhood, and cement your average good guy credentials by saving the day.

How to Fix a Flat Tire

Some heroes hide behind a secret identity. For Superman, putting on glasses and acting like a forgettable nebbish is a way to live a somewhat normal life—and also to masquerade as a reporter and get up-to-date news about disasters as they happen so he can save the day as Superman. But sometimes Clark Kent is put in situations where he can't use Superman's powers to easily solve problems. A stranded motorist, for example, is bound to notice if he shoots laser beams from his eyes to seal a punctured tire. Clark Kent has to know how to do things the old-fashioned way. Luckily, fixing a tire is not that complicated, and if you follow these steps, you too will end up looking pretty super to the driver you help back onto the road.

Step 1: Turn on the hazard lights.
It's important to let passing traffic know that the vehicle is experiencing technical difficulties. When they see the car's hazard lights, alert drivers will give the vehicle a wide berth. (If you've stopped to help a stranded motorist, go directly to step 3.)

Step 2: Pull off on a flat and level surface away from traffic.
If you're a passenger in a car that develops a flat, calmly direct the driver to a convenient place to change the tire. Most modern cars can drive on a single flat for a short distance at low speed without damaging the wheel rim. Stop where there's a level surface that is flat and hard enough to support a jack without sinking into the ground. The side of the road is ideal, as long as you're a sufficient distance from passing traffic. Once parked, have the driver turn off the engine, set the parking brake, and remove the keys from the ignition.

Step 3: Evacuate the vehicle.
All passengers should exit the vehicle and stand at a safe distance away from traffic.

Step 4: Remove the jack, spare tire, and tools from the trunk.
If the car is modern, all the relevant tools to fix a flat should be stored beneath the

cover in the trunk or hatch, including the jack and jack handle, lug wrench, and spare tire.

 Some vehicles come equipped with a temporary spare tire commonly called a donut, which is thinner than a standard tire. The donut is designed to get you on your way and should be used only long enough to drive to a garage or tire repair shop. It should not be used as a replacement tire.

Step 5: Block the wheel diagonal to your flat.
With a rock, block the front of the tire diagonal to the flat tire. If blocking a front tire, wedge the block in front of the tire. If blocking a rear tire, place the block behind the tire. This will prevent the vehicle from rolling as it's jacked up.

Step 6: Remove the wheel cover (if any).
Using the beveled end of the lug wrench, pry off the wheel cover by inserting the wrench firmly between the cover and the wheel and pushing it toward the vehicle. Work your way around the cover if necessary to pry it loose.

Step 7: Loosen the lug nuts.
With the wrench end of the lug wrench, loosen each lug nut with a single counterclockwise turn. Do not remove the lug nuts completely until the vehicle has been jacked up.

Step 8: Place the jack in position.
If changing a front tire, place the jack behind the tire so that it will lift the solid frame or undercarriage of the vehicle. If changing a rear tire, the jack should be placed in front of the tire to lift the frame or undercarriage. Do not place the jack under a front or rear bumper; neither will likely support the weight of the jacked vehicle, which could slip and fall on you. Also, it's important to have the jack situated on a solid surface. Loose soil or mud will cause the jack to push into the ground rather than lift the vehicle.

Step 9: Jack the car up.

Insert the jack handle into the jack, and either turn it clockwise or pump it (depending on the jack) to lift the vehicle clear of the ground. Raising it by less than an inch (2.5 cm) is preferable, so that if the car accidentally falls, the risk of damage to it or injury to you is minimal.

Step 10: Remove the lug nuts and the wheel.

With the lug wrench, turn the lugs counterclockwise to remove them completely. Then grip the wheel with both hands, and pull it straight off the lug bolts; set the flat aside.

Step 11: Install the spare tire.

Mount the spare tire, securing it in place with the lug nuts. Screw the nuts by hand. You'll tighten the lugs with the lug wrench once the vehicle is lowered.

Step 12: Lower the vehicle.

Turn the jack handle counterclockwise to lower the vehicle back to the ground. If it's a pump-action jack, lift the handle up, and hold it until the vehicle is slowly lowered.

Step 13: Tighten the lug nuts, and replace the wheel cover.

Use the lug wrench to tighten the lug nuts fully, and then replace the wheel cover, pressing it in place using the heel of your hand. Gather up the flat tire and tools, and return them to the trunk.

How to Jumpstart a Car

If Clark Kent is stopped on the streets of Metropolis by a motorist who needs help jumpstarting his car, Clark does not run off and then return to the scene as Superman. He follows the exact same steps the average good guy would go through to help out. Superman may be a living solar battery, but he can't muster up an electric jolt to recharge a battery. Luckily, jumpstarting a car is quick and easy—all you need is a set of jumper cables and a working battery that's the same voltage as the dead battery.

Step 1: Pull your car adjacent to or in front of the car you will assist, grille to grille.
Be sure that the cars are not in contact with each other. Turn off the ignitions in both vehicles.

Step 2: Identify all the connection sites.
All car batteries and jumper cables are clearly marked. A plus sign (+), the word *POS*, or the color red denotes the positive end of the jumper cables. Conversely, a negative sign (–), *NEG*, or the color black denotes the negative end of the cables. Similarly, car battery terminals will be marked with plus and minus signs to indicate the respective positive and negative terminals.

Step 3: Connect the jumper cables from the dead battery to the live battery.
Connect the jumper cable's positive clamp to the positive terminal of the dead battery. Then connect the second positive clamp of your jumper cable to the positive terminal of the vehicle with the live battery. Next, connect the jumper cable's negative clamp to the negative terminal of the vehicle with the live battery. Then connect the second negative clamp of your jumper cable to the engine block of the vehicle with the dead battery, thus grounding the connection.

Before you connect cables to batteries, remember that batteries contain sulfuric acid and explosive gases. Damaged or frozen batteries should never be jumpstarted. And you should never lean over a battery when connecting or disconnecting cables. Batteries can explode, spraying sulfuric acid that can severely damage your skin and eyes and necessitate immediate medical attention. If you do receive a splash of battery acid in the eyes, immediately flush the exposed tissue with clean water and seek medical attention.

Step 4: Ensure that the jumper cables are clear of any obstruction.
Be attentive to the location of fans or belts. Make sure there is nothing that could sever one of the cables when the cars are turned on.

Step 5: Start the cars, live-battery vehicle first.
Start your car first, then start the car with the dead battery. Your car's battery should provide enough charge to start the stalled vehicle. Leave both cars running for a maximum duration of 15 minutes to charge the dead battery.

Step 6: Remove the jumper cable clamps.
Once the stalled engine is idling, remove the jumper cables in the reverse order that they were attached. The negative clamp attached to the engine block of the rescued vehicle should be removed first, followed by the negative clamp on your car. Then remove the positive clamp from your car, followed by the positive clamp on the rescued vehicle. Once the latter vehicle is running, its alternator should do the work of fully recharging the battery.

How to Put Out a Fire

Putting out fires is a standard part of Superman's rescuing duties. Superman has a number of ways to deal with a runaway blaze. He can extinguish raging forest fires with a frigid gust of his super-breath. He can simply inhale the flames into his invulnerable lungs. He can even spin in place at superspeed to create a vacuum to suck out all the oxygen feeding an inferno. But if he's stuck at the *Daily Planet* in disguise as Clark Kent, faced with the kind of trashcan fire for which superpowers might be overkill, it's probably easier for him to grab a nearby fire extinguisher. The average good guy can do the same thing, but it's a big help to know the types of fire extinguishers and which are best suited to a particular blaze.

When using extinguishers, stand a safe 10 to 15 feet (3–4.5 m) away as you deploy the extinguisher's contents over the flames and smoldering material. Most extinguishers are designed with an easy squeeze toggle to activate. Simply point and spray.

Before trying to put out a fire, first alert professional firefighters by calling emergency services or activating a building's fire alarm. Often, sprinklers or other automatic extinguishing measures will do the job for you. Only tackle fires that aren't raging out of control. Before even thinking of battling a blaze, you should evacuate any potential victims. Saving lives always trumps saving personal property. Buildings can be rebuilt.

Technique 1: ABC dry chemical extinguisher.

ABC extinguishers are rated for fires involving combustible materials such as wood or cloth or flammable liquids (gasoline, kerosene, paint thinners). For fires in small electrical or electronic equipment, unplug the equipment first: The fire is likely fed by sparking electricity and once deprived of power will usually extinguish in short order. Use the ABC extinguisher to put out any additional flames or smoldering material.

Technique 2: D-rated extinguisher.

Combustible metals such as sodium, potassium, magnesium, or titanium, which burn at very high temperatures, require this type of extinguisher.

Technique 3: Dry chemical, halon, or CO_2 extinguishers.

These fire extinguishers are typically used to combat small structural fires in homes or other buildings that have not become completely engulfed in flames. Always read the directions of any fire extinguisher before deploying. Home-based fire extinguishers should be checked regularly to make sure the units are charged and ready for use at a moment's notice.

Technique 4: Pressurized water hoses.

Water under pressure from a fire company tanker truck or fueled by a streetside fire hydrant is the tried-and-true way to combat a raging fire threatening a dwelling or business.

Technique 5: K extinguisher.

Mixing water and potassium acetate, the K extinguisher is used specifically to battle grease fires in restaurants.

Technique 6: Foam extinguisher.

Designed to fight gasoline fires, AFFF, or protein foam, extinguishers are preferred over water hoses because pressurized water simply scatters gas fires. Made of 3 or 6 percent foam mixed with 97 or 94 percent water, the foam extinguisher coats flaming gasoline with an emulsifying agent that stops oxygen from fueling the fire, thus smothering it out entirely.

How to Deal with a Gas Leak

Metropolis would probably be a much safer city without S.T.A.R. Labs. Scientific and Technological Advanced Research Laboratories has its most ambitious facility in Metropolis. Its scientists' cutting-edge research into new fields has helped Superman numerous times—but a number of experiments there have also gone very wrong, leading to a number of superpowered monsters rampaging across the city. While your place of employment is probably nowhere near as dangerous as S.T.A.R. Labs, there are still common dangers to look out for at work, such as a gas leak. Gas leaks can also strike at home, especially if you have a gas stove. Natural gas leaks can be deadly in several ways, suffocating silently or building up to levels that explode in fiery fury with just the smallest spark. The Man of Steel could simply inhale a cloud of gas and super-compress it in his lungs, then fly to a safe area for exhalation and dispersal. But the average good guy should bear in mind that getting himself and any potential victims out of the area is the main way to help others in the event of a natural gas leak.

Step 1: Know the warning signs.

Companies that bottle and distribute natural gas add the chemical mercaptin to produce the recognizable rotten-egg smell associated with it. If you get a faint whiff of this telltale odor, first check the pilot lights or burner valves on gas furnaces or stoves. The odor may be caused by an extinguished pilot light, which can easily be remedied by relighting it. A burner valve left partially open may be leaking gas. If the smell is still apparent after relighting the pilot or turning off the valves completely, call your utility company for immediate service, and proceed to step 2.

Step 2: Evacuate the premises immediately.

The most important thing is to have everyone leave the area affected by the gas smell as quickly as possible to avoid injury.

Step 3: Do not switch on lights or any other electrical equipment.

If the gas buildup is sufficient to emit a very strong odor, it may also cause an explosion if ignited by the slightest spark. So don't turn on any lights to illuminate your way or make any telephone calls from within the premises. Just focus on evacuating yourself and anyone else inside.

Step 4: Don't worry about ventilating the premises.

With natural gas buildups, the natural inclination is to attempt to ventilate the affected area by opening windows or doors. But a stuck metal latch on a window or door hasp could spark if scraped open, causing an explosion. Just exit the area immediately. It's okay to leave doors open as you leave, but the paramount priority is to get out as quickly as you can.

Step 5: Once everyone is safely away, call emergency services if you haven't already.

After you've exited and are safely removed from the gas buildup, it's safe to use a cellular phone or a neighbor's telephone to call emergency services, which will alert the utility company. Additionally, the local fire company may respond just to be on hand in the event of a possible explosion or fire. Once the gas leak is capped and the premises are sufficiently ventilated, it should be safe to return.

SUPER-SANCTUARY

There's no place like home. But a good guy's private dwelling may not be the refuge he needs to rest and relax between rescues, especially if he has to preserve his all-important secret identity. For a super hero, a secret sanctuary can be that home away from home. Batman has his Batcave, and Superman has his Fortress of Solitude. This secret headquarters houses surviving relics of Krypton and other wonders—it's also the one place the Man of Steel can go when he needs to get away from it all. Originally, the Fortress was hidden away in the snow-covered Arctic and locked tight with a giant arrow-shaped key only the Man of Steel could lift. Later, Superman moved the Fortress into a tesseract sphere that he could balance on one finger. The tesseract allowed the Fortress to exist in another dimension, accessed only through the sphere, which Superman hid on a remote mountaintop. More recently, a new and quite inaccessible Fortress exists deep in the Amazon rainforest within Maya temple ruins. Here is a list of some of the unique rooms and features that have existed in the Fortresses of Solitude, past to present.

Kryptonian Relics
Artifacts from Superman's home planet Krypton include a working Kryptonian warsuit (battle armor); a crystalline diorama of Krypton's capital, Kryptonopolis; a facsimile of an elegant Kryptonian skyship; and a Krypton memorial featuring realistic statues of Superman's biological parents, Jor-El and Lara Lor-Van.

Phantom Zone Generator
This soliton generator provides access to the so-called Phantom Zone, a limbo-like area of extradimensional space once used to imprison Kryptonian criminals.

Trophy Room
This room includes the coils of Superman's foe Conduit, a model of the helicopter the Man of Steel saved from crashing in his very first adventure, and various relics from Superman's past victories, along with a holographic archive of his adventures.

Kelex
The advanced robot majordomo in charge of the Fortress's care and upkeep is an exact duplicate of the robot that performed similar duties on Krypton for Jor-El.

Journal of Silas Kent
This personal account chronicles the Kents' migration to Kansas and parts west during America's tumultuous nineteenth century.

Control Hub
A bank of ever-vigilant computers in the communications room helps the Man of Steel keep watch over Earth.

Interplanetary Zoo
Superman once maintained this galactic Noah's Ark for alien species whose natural homes or environments were destroyed or rendered uninhabitable.

Slag Pool
A molten bath is used by the Man of Steel to cleanse his body of alien microorganisms and other contaminants; it is also used to disintegrate dangerous materials.

Kandor
The "bottle city" was, in fact, a real alien metropolis shrunken and stolen by the villain known as Tolos. Superman keeps Kandor safe until he can restore the city to its full size.

Krypto's Kennel
The Super-Dog's home was specially built from toughened materials. In Superman's absence, Krypto was cared for by the Superman-Robot known as Ned.

Kryptonian warsuit for especially dangerous rescues

Memorial to Superman's parents, for inspiration

Control hub monitoring for worldwide emergencies

The bottle city of Kandor

Kelex, faithful robot servant

Spectral nexus apparatus, generating the tesseract around the Fortress

Holographic info bank on super-villains

Reports on past exploits

Kryptonite sample, under heavy shielding

How to Refill
a Water Cooler

Clark Kent's ability to blend in goes further than just slapping on a pair of glasses. He's the kind of quiet, dependable employee who isn't very interesting to gossip about. You too can escape the often sharp eyes and tongues of co-workers by just being the nice person in the office—for instance, the person who refills the water cooler, a task that makes most people flee the premises. Just as Clark Kent is the guy who quietly replenishes the *Daily Planet's* water cooler, the average good guy isn't afraid of a little splashed water.

Step 1: Remove the empty water bottle.
Simply lift the empty container from the top of the water cooler. The reservoir at the top of the cooler doesn't need to be empty of water. In fact, you should always leave a little water in the reservoir, particularly in coolers that offer both hot and cold water, so that the internal heating element doesn't burn out.

Step 2: Ready the new bottle for insertion by removing the plastic cap, if necessary, and wiping off the top of the bottle.
A 5-gallon (19-l) bottle of water, standard for most office water coolers, weighs approximately 42 pounds (19 kg). While it's a burden that doesn't require super-strength to handle, it can be awkward to lift, and you'll need to lift it well above your waist to insert it into the waiting water cooler.

Step 3: Lift the bottle onto a nearby chair.
For ease in lifting, place a sturdy chair next to the cooler, and lift the bottle onto it first. Remember to lift with your legs and not your back to avoid muscle strain.

Step 4: Tilt the bottle's open end over the reservoir, and set it in place.
Water will pour from the open bottle, so you'll need to set it in place quickly to avoid excess spillage. Don't panic, however—there is time enough to pour the water in without the entire mechanism overflowing.

Many current water cooler models feature reservoirs tipped with prongs that puncture the factory seal of the refill bottle's cap—there is no need to remove the cap beforehand. This new design is favorable because it's more sanitary and minimizes spilling. Of course, if you spill, the good guy thing to do is to clean up the mess.

SUPER-MAKEOVER

Only an invulnerable Man of Steel, impervious to heat and humidity, could wear a business suit through the hottest months in Metropolis without breaking a sweat, not to mention wearing an entire costume beneath it. More than a fashion choice, Clark Kent's attire conceals his identity and helps him masquerade as a mild-mannered reporter for a major metropolitan newspaper. Thanks to some clever tailoring, the Man of Tomorrow can also wear his special costume beneath his clothing to enable lightning-quick changes when he's called to action.

Spit Curl
Normally, Superman's hair is parted on his left side, his forelocks falling in a natural "spit curl" that is as identifiable and unique to him as the stylized S symbol he wears on his chest. As Clark Kent, the Man of Steel slicks back his hair for a more conservative look. Clark smiles more easily than Superman, whose face carries a more stoic and serious countenance.

Spectacles
Once upon a time, the lenses of Clark's eyeglasses were made from broken fragments of the canopy to his Kryptonian rocket. The glass—in small pieces but still indestructible—could therefore withstand the extremely high temperatures generated by Clark's heat vision if he were forced to clandestinely use that particular power. More recently, Clark keeps identical extra copies of his glasses on hand, the spectacles softening Superman's chiseled features and making Clark look more bookwormish.

Business Suit
Growing up on a Kansas farm made Clark penny wise but not pound foolish. His suits may look professionally tailored but are, in fact, from Metropolis department stores. Ma Kent's skills with needle and thread help Clark to wear the suits a trifle larger to accommodate Superman's costume worn beneath. Thus, the broad-shouldered and heavily muscled hero is able to conceal his physique by looking more nondescript than husky. Clark's button-down shirts, however, are specially purchased triple-weave cotton that leave no hint that he's wearing his colorful uniform underneath.

Power Tie

Clark's silk ties complement his suits nicely without being too ostentatious or calling attention to the wearer. While the Man of Steel can tie and untie a standard necktie at superspeed, he often wears clip-on ties for expediency in changing into his "working clothes."

Big Shoes

Clark wears his wingtip shoes a size and a half larger to accommodate Superman's red boots beneath.

Briefcase

Although his cape can be folded inconspicuously beneath his suit, unfurling dramatically as Clark doffs his coat and shirt to reveal the S shield beneath, occasionally he detaches the crimson cloak and stores it within a hidden compartment in his briefcase. Or, when following a hot story, the cape can be stored in a similarly stealthy pocket in Clark's shoulder bag.

Clark's glasses obscure Superman's distinctive eyes.

Clark Kent's hair is slicked back and conservative.

Clark has a relaxed smile.

Clark is careful to wear nondescript ties that don't draw attention to him.

Clark's suit is oversized to hide his physique and allow his costume to fit beneath it.

Sometimes Clark hides Superman's cape in a secret compartment in his briefcase.

Clark wears large shoes to accommodate Superman's boots within them.

How to Repair a Broken Photocopier

Newspapers like the *Daily Planet* run on giant rolls of newsprint, but the offices rely on a constant flow of printed material from photocopiers. Unfortunately, as anyone who has used a photocopier in an office knows, they all work perfectly—at least 80 percent of the time. They spend the remainder of their life sitting quietly, possibly beeping, as paper sits jammed deep within them. Superman, however, has faced far worse machines—Brainiac and Metallo—and is unafraid of the photocopiers at the *Daily Planet*. And you shouldn't fear the ones in your workplace either. Care and maintenance of a copying machine is relatively easy, and you don't need to be a Man of Steel to troubleshoot the usual problems associated with the average office copier.

Step 1: Read the copier's handbook.
Anyone using the photocopier regularly should read the handbook provided by the manufacturer for use and minor maintenance directions.

Step 2: Check the control panel.
Most new photocopiers feature digital control panels with light-up displays that track the inner workings of the unit. These panels will not only tell you what the problem is and where on the machine to look, but they'll also often explain how to fix it. Check the digital panel on your photocopier before you proceed with any other troubleshooting. Most of the issues you will face will be diagnosed here, including the three most common and easily diagnosed problems: paper jams, low toner, and empty paper trays.

Step 3: Check to see if there is a paper jam.
Paper fed through the transition or exit rollers of a copier will occasionally get caught in the copier's inner mechanics, crumpling up or shredding entirely and causing the copier to jam. Copiers are designed to shut down when a jam occurs to prevent damage to the machine. Your control panel will show where the jam

has taken place. Open the copier's casing at the designated point, and pull out the offending paper. Make sure to remove all bits of paper—any remaining scraps could cause further jams or even damage the offset drums that transmit images to paper, a costly and time-consuming repair job. Do not use sharp metal objects to dig out jams, and don't touch any of the internal circuitry. You risk electrocution from the high-voltage electronics within the machine.

Step 4: Replace the toner.
Practically all modern copiers will shut down before they run out of toner to avoid wasting paper. The control panel will light up and tell you when the machine's toner level is too low. Copier toner is a very fine dust-like substance contained in plastic cartridges or bottles. Consult the unit's handbook for instructions for replacing the toner cartridge, and use only manufacturer-recommended toner specific to the unit you're servicing. Toner not recommended for your machine could damage or destroy the copier and should always be avoided. If you get toner on your clothing, immediately wash the item in cold water to avoid permanent staining.

Step 5: Refill the paper trays.
Just as a lack of toner will shut down the machine until the toner is replenished, many copiers will not operate if the paper trays feeding the unit are empty. Again, low or empty paper trays will usually be indicated on your copier's display panel. Simply consult the handbook for proper replacement procedure, and use only recommended paper sizes and weights.

Step 6: If all else fails, check the plug and call a repair person.
If toner and paper are plentiful and there are no jams indicated, check the plug. Often enough, a pulled plug can be the culprit, especially if no indicator lights are lit. If your copier has power and still isn't working, you should call a trained repair person.

SUPER-ALTEREGO

Most people get it backward: Mild-mannered reporter Clark Kent existed long before Superman—not to mention Kal-El of Krypton preceding them both—so the Man of Steel is really the secret identity of Clark, not vice versa. However, for super heroes, the civilian alter ego is generally regarded as the "secret" that must be carefully guarded for several important reasons. As Superman would be the first to attest, maintaining a secret identity has both benefits and detriments, including the following.

PRO: Superman 24/7

The Man of Steel once attempted to operate as a hero full-time, abandoning his life as Clark Kent entirely. However, the pressures of such an undertaking soon took their toll, and Superman realized that being Clark Kent in his "off time" enabled him to rest and relax. Even the world's greatest hero needs some time off.

CON: Secrets and Lies

For a stalwart Man of Steel raised on the values of virtue and honesty, keeping his secret identity secret involves deceiving the people he cares about most, who may suspect that Clark and Superman are one and the same.

PRO: Safety

Superman would gladly share his secret with the world as a sign of his total devotion to heroism, but such a revelation would put his loved ones at risk. Armed with such knowledge, Superman's many enemies would gladly strike at Lois Lane or his parents, the Kents. To protect his family and friends, Superman must forever keep his true identity hidden from the world.

CON: Logistics

Part of the problem in having dual identities is explaining where you've been and what you've been doing to employers or colleagues. While some might get fired for having so many unexplained absences, Clark Kent picked the perfect career. As a reporter for the *Daily Planet*, he's often called away to chronicle the news of the day. Superman has the good fortune of being able to come and go at superspeed, catching up on work similarly to beat the clock.

How to Fix a Burst Pipe

Growing up in Smallville, Kansas, and enduring cold Midwestern winters, Clark Kent knows well the troubles associated with frozen and burst water pipes. And because he did not arrive on Earth with his superpowers fully developed, he had to learn some handy plumbing skills early on to prevent water damage to the Kents' farmhouse. While superpowers can definitely help with a plumbing disaster, the average plumber manages to make it without super-cold breath or X-ray vision, which means there's hope for the average good guy to save the day, too.

Step 1: Find the leak.

Many leaks begin with frozen pipes. When water freezes from liquid to ice, it expands by 10 percent. In an enclosed pipe, the ice will test the expansion limits of the metal or plastic of the piping. This internal stress will often wrench a pipe from a joint or burst the pipe itself. The resulting leak may begin as a slow drip but end up a pressurized gusher if not repaired quickly, especially once the ice thaws and the water returns to pressure. Obviously, the first order of business is to find the leak: Look for a drip, spray, or outpouring of water, depending on how badly the pipe is burst. Grab a bucket to catch the overflow.

Step 2: Turn off the water supply, and drain the burst pipe.

Most burst pipes occur in basements, which are often unheated and where temperatures in cold climates drop significantly during winter months. Turn off your water supply at the central valve so that you don't inundate your basement any further (see How to Dry Out a Flooded Basement, page 173). Allow the burst pipe to drain, and remove any belongings from the flooded area.

Step 3: Cut out the burst section of pipe.

Use a pipe cutter or hacksaw to remove the section of burst pipe. (Do not cut a lead pipe. Many older homes still have lead plumbing, now prohibited for sale because of the many health concerns associated with lead. A burst lead pipe is a good opportunity to take the drastic—and often expensive—step of hiring a professional to replace your entire plumbing system, or at the very least the pipes supplying drinking and bathing water, to avoid the health effects of lead exposure.) Be sure to remove the entire burst section, including any distorted lengths. If you use a hacksaw, you may need to file down any metal or plastic burrs on the pipe's severed edges so that a repair pipe can be easily slid into place over both exposed ends and secured.

Step 4: Replace the removed section with a slip-on coupling or push-fit repair pipe.
The replacement pipe should slide into place between the two severed pipes, with the edges of the severed pipes fitting inside the replacement pipe. For copper pipes, a slip-on coupling will fit over the existing pipe ends and secure (and seal) both ends with an olive (a brass ring) and nut. Tighten the nut with your fingers, and then use a wrench to tighten it further and prevent potential leaks. The olive between the nut and the coupling on both ends of the repair pipe will compress to form a watertight seal. Plastic pipes can be repaired with a similar slip-on coupling plus a waterproof sealer epoxy. "Paint" the epoxy inside a single nut on each end, as well as around the edges of the existing pipe; when dry, the epoxy will seal the pipe. For both copper and plastic pipes, you can also use a push-fit system, basically a ready-made repair kit featuring a flexible pipe that is inserted over either end of the pipe being repaired. Simply tighten down the new pipe with a nut and olive, or cement it into place with epoxy to make it watertight. If you use epoxies or other plastic sealers, allow ample time to dry before testing the repaired pipe.

Step 5: Restore water.
After you've repaired the pipe and allowed the epoxy or sealer time to dry, turn your water supply back on, and let the water recirculate throughout the plumbing system. You may need to turn on a faucet serviced by the repaired pipe to draw water back into it. Once you know water is running through the pipe, turn the faucet off so that the pipe remains under constant water pressure. If you repaired the pipe properly, there should be no further leaks. If water dribbles from the coupling ends, use a wrench to tighten the nuts further until the drips stop. Keep an eye on the repaired pipe for several days to make certain that your repair is a success.

You don't always need X-ray vision to identify the pipe that's leaking.

Clark Kent has shut off the water so he can repair the pipe.

Clark slips on a coupling to the pipe ends, along with an olive and nut on both sides.

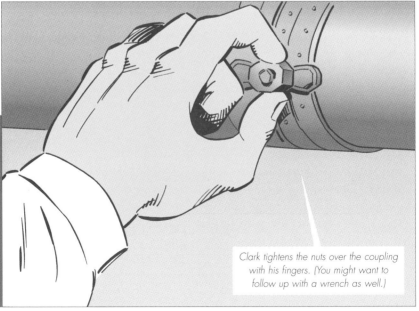

Clark tightens the nuts over the coupling with his fingers. (You might want to follow up with a wrench as well.)

How to Dry Out a Flooded Basement

While Jonathan and Martha Kent probably got a little worried when their son started developing the ability to lift tractors and fly, they also were unlikely to regret the day he discovered he could simply suck up all the water in a flooded basement into his super-lungs and then spew it out and irrigate acres of farmland in a few moments. But before that truly historic day, Clark and his parents had to follow a few more ordinary steps to clear out their basement when it was inundated with floodwater or the outpouring of a burst pipe. The average good guy can accomplish such a task with a portable pump and commonly available cleaning supplies.

Step 1: Turn off all electrical and gas utilities.
Before you enter a flooded basement, make sure all electricity and natural gas outlets are turned off to prevent short-outs, electrocution, or buildups of flammable gases.

Step 2: Examine outside walls for structural damage.
A basement flooded from a broken or burst pipe is preferable to one knee-deep in floodwater. Floodwater from torrential rains or overflowing rivers can pour in through low casement windows or rise up from basement drains with nowhere else to go. These waters are dirty and often laden with raw sewage or other contaminants. Furthermore, these rushing waters can cause damage to the structural integrity of your basement's foundation. Before entering a flooded basement, you should make certain that there's no danger of collapse.

Step 3: Take photos or video of the flooded basement for insurance purposes.
A pictorial record of the damage your home suffered will help you receive swift reimbursement from your insurance company to cover the costs of repairs.

Step 4: Open any doors and windows to begin drying out.
If the basement is wet as a result of outside flooding, don gloves and wading boots before entering the standing water, which may be contaminated with waste

products. Then open any doors and windows to allow humidity to escape and drier air to circulate.

Step 5: Begin pumping out standing water.
A gas-powered pump will quickly remove the floodwater, assuming that flooding has receded from outside the house's foundation. Pump the water out in stages to avoid structural damage to the saturated foundation, removing only one-third of the total volume each day. If floodwaters outside have not receded, you risk collapsing the foundation, since water pressure exerted from outside is only held back by the water volume inside the foundation. Make sure that your pump hoses lead well away from the foundation so that what you pump out doesn't flood back in. Mark the receding waters on the basement walls to measure the effectiveness of your pump. Marks on the walls also help make clear any possible reflooding. There's no point in drying out if the flood danger persists.

Step 6: Sanitize the basement.
Once the basement is clear of standing water, shovel out any debris that may have been carried into the basement. Then sanitize the walls, floor, and any salvageable items with an antibacterial detergent or bleach solution.

Step 7: Restore power, and set up a dehumidifier.
A small dehumidifier, if left to operate for several days, should be all you'll need to remove excess humidity from the air and dry out the basement. Empty the unit's catch basin regularly.

Step 8: Repair any structural damage to the floor or foundation.
The force of incoming floodwater can cause concrete foundations to buckle and heave. Floors can be similarly displaced. You may have to repair small to significant cracks in both or even lay down entirely new concrete to reseal your basement. Once the repairs are completed, look into ways to prevent future flooding. One method is to install drainage pipes below the surface of the earth around your foundation, diverting water away from your house. Another tactic is to dig a swail—a gently sloping drainage ditch—to divert large amounts of runoff water away from your house and other structures. Typically, swails are covered with grass or vegetation.

How to Fix an Electrical Outage

Superman and Lois Lane have had a complicated relationship, and in some ways it's hard to imagine their life as a married couple. Does Lois cook a turkey in the oven, or does Clark just blink at it with his heat vision? And what happens when the power goes out? Lois is incredibly self-sufficient, but when something goes wrong around the house, it's a safe bet that Superman will make everything right. If your power goes out, you won't need super-powers to fix it. Home power outages often involve a tripped circuit breaker or blown fuse, either of which can be easily fixed by the average good guy if he knows just what to do.

Step 1: Check lights and appliances.

If the street lights are out, chances are your entire neighborhood is suffering a blackout. All you can do is wait for the power grid to be repaired and electricity restored. But if you check the lights and appliances in your home and find that only some areas lack power, you've likely blown a fuse or tripped your circuit breaker.

Step 2: Disconnect or turn off affected lights or appliances.

To prevent a power surge, disconnect any appliances or lights affected by the outage. Circuit breakers are often tripped or fuses blown by overloaded outlets or defective appliances. By disconnecting, you prevent the circuit breaker from tripping again or a new fuse from blowing once you've reset your home's electrical system.

Step 3: Go to your home's breaker box.

The electrical systems in practically all modern homes and apartments are controlled by breaker boxes with circuits or fuses keyed to specific "zones" of electricity, usually room by room. Go to your breaker box, usually found in your basement or on the first floor. Make sure you have dry hands before opening the box. Stand on a rubber pad or dry wooden board so that you ground yourself. You should open the breaker's main switch to cut off power as you reset the tripped breaker or replace any blown fuses. Resetting a tripped breaker is simply a matter of throwing the switch or handle fully to its OFF position and then returning it to the ON position, which should restore power immediately if no other wiring or electrical systems are compromised.

Step 4: Look for blown fuses in the zone affected by the outage.
You can easily recognize a blown fuse by its cloudy or blackened glass. Remove the fuse by unscrewing it or pulling it out (if it is a cartridge-type fuse), and throw it away. Only use a same-sized fuse when replacing blown fuses. Never try to extend the life of a blown fuse or restore a circuit by placing a copper penny behind it to complete the circuit. While power will flow through this makeshift circuit, a viable fuse serves to regulate the flow of electricity, which is unchecked by the copper penny. You could blow your entire electrical system or cause a fire with this cheap solution. Don't be frugal. Save the penny, and spend a few dollars more for the required fuse.

Step 5: Restore power.
Once you replace the fuse, close the main switch again to restore power to your home. Avoid overloading outlets or using a particular faulty appliance that may have caused the outage in the first place. Repair or replace faulty appliances; they can also be fire and electrocution hazards.

WHO KNOWS SUPERMAN'S SECRET?

While Superman's secret identity has served him well in many ways, it's a hard secret to keep. It's not a surprise that his parents and Lois Lane know about his double life, but unfortunately, there are more people in on the secret than you might think. The following is a short list of the friends (and foes) who know that Clark Kent is actually the Man of Steel.

Jonathan and Martha Kent
Clark's parents were the first to know, helping their super-son concoct his heroic alterego.

Lois Lane
Lois always had an inkling but was taken completely by surprise when Clark eventually won her heart over the Man of Steel and then revealed that the two men were one and the same.

Lana Lang
Clark's childhood sweetheart figured it out and kept the knowledge to herself for years to protect him.

Batman
Superman's closest super hero friend knows the truth. Just try keeping a secret like this from the world's greatest detective. Of course, Superman also knows that Batman masquerades as billionaire playboy Bruce Wayne.

JLA
While not every member of the Justice League of America is in the know, the main seven permanent members know that their teammate moonlights as Clark Kent. In addition to the aforementioned Dark Knight, those in the know include Aquaman, the Flash, Green Lantern, the Martian Manhunter, and Wonder Woman.

Conduit
Kenny Braverman, a jealous pal of the teenage Clark in Smallville, figured out Superman's secret identity. As an adult, Kenny became the villain Conduit and nearly destroyed Clark and the Kents in vicious attacks that ended in his

own demise. Conduit took Clark's secret to the grave.

Jimmy Olsen?

Nope! Ironically, Superman's best friend isn't privy to his secret identity. Ah, the hardships of being Jimmy.

How to Save a Kitten Stuck in a Tree

While stopping homicidal maniacs and saving the world are among Superman's greatest feats, it's often the time he takes to help others that leaves the biggest impression. While Superman can simply fly up and grab a cat stuck in a tree, the average good guy can accomplish the same rescue with nothing more than a can of cat food or a tall ladder. Most fire companies no longer respond to calls involving cats stuck in trees, on telephone poles, or on other high perches, so it's up to you to save the day.

Step 1: Wait it out.
If confronted by such a kitty conundrum, first consider waiting it out. The cat will likely come down eventually, unless it climbs to a height from which it might be too scared to descend.

Step 2: Entice it with food.
Hunger is a great motivator, especially for a kitten that has been perched in a tree for several hours. Just place a can of cat food or tuna under the tree or pole, and wait for the kitten to climb down. A tame house cat may come down more quickly than a feral cat that is wary of human contact. You may have to leave the can of food and move away from the tree and out of a skittish cat's sight so that she'll feel comfortable enough to climb down.

Step 3: Get a tall ladder.
If the kitten is too frightened to climb down, even for food, find a ladder of suitable height and climb it to retrieve her. Have someone hold the base of the ladder steady, especially when you near the cat and face the precarious task of grabbing hold of an animal that may scratch or bite in defense. For this reason, wear heavy work gloves or garden gloves. Climb past the kitten so that her first inclination isn't to climb farther up the tree. In fact, your very presence may leave her no alternative but to make her own descent.

Step 4: Grab and hold tight.

A tame cat that knows you might jump into your arms with a friendly purr. More likely, you will face a hissing cat with raised hackles. Carefully grab the cat by the scruff of her neck and hold tight. Gripped in this position, she shouldn't be able to bite or claw you. The cat may thrash, necessitating a firm grip. An alternative is to use a net that's strong enough to hold a cat, with holes smaller than a standard fishing net. You don't want a cat slicing her way free of a net high above the ground.

Step 5: Climb down.

The tricky part is climbing down with one hand clutching a thrashing kitten and the other clinging to the ladder's rungs. Tread carefully so you don't fall and don't drop the kitten. Once you're close to the ground, let the cat down or pass her off to the person holding the ladder so that you can complete the climb down safely.

Acknowledgments

First and foremost, thanks to Superman for setting the standard and raising the bar for every super hero—real or imagined—to follow.

Extra-special thanks to editors John Morgan and John W. Glenn, for patience and understanding above and beyond the call of duty.

Thanks to Quirk Books' David Borgenicht, Jason Rekulak, and Mike Rogalski, as well as DC Comics' Steve Korté.

Super-thanks to Mark Waid, whose Kryptonian knowledge and understanding of the Man of Steel are unassailable.

Thanks to my good friend, Chuck Dixon, always fast on the draw for names and lists.

Thanks to illustrious illustrators John Delaney, Dave Cooper, and Terry Beatty.

Thanks to Ted Fisher and Dr. Gary Bonfante, D.O., real-life heroes who I'm happy to call friends.

Thanks to the following for their expertise in explaining how (both in theory and practice) to save lives and be an ultimate good guy (or gal): Kristin Almasi and the Humane Society of Lackawanna County; Stephanie Berger, The American Foundation for Suicide Prevention; Susan Calantoni, M.S., CCC-A; Sue Davis of Crystal Springs Water; Rafael Delgado of Kombat Arts Training Academy; Guinness World Records; Bill Hunsinger of Four-Star Business Systems; Deborah Leuffen of UGI Utilities; Dr. Brian Willard; Teressa Withers; and all the individuals (especially the anonymous firefighters of the Lehigh Valley) who contributed invaluable information but prefer to preserve their secret identities.

And thanks to Jennifer Myskowski, Finnegan Beatty, and Wilbur the Super-Dog.

About the Super-Crew

Scott Beatty is also the author of *The Batman Handbook* (Quirk 2005) as well as *Superman: The Ultimate Guide to the Man of Steel*. Scott's DC Comics credits include the recent sold-out *Nightwing Year One* miniseries, in which the Last Son of Krypton made an inspiring cameo appearance. To date, Scott has exhibited no unique superpowers under the rays of Earth's yellow star except an inclination to sunburn. Scott's Fortress of Solitude is secreted somewhere in the woods of Northeastern Pennsylvania.

John Delaney is an award-winning storyboard artist, animator, and comic book artist with more than 20 years of experience in both live action production and animation. For the past 12 years, John has worked as a comic book artist for DC Comics and Bongo Comics. He has penciled a wide variety of characters, such as Superman, Batman, Wonder Woman, the Justice League, Dexter's Laboratory, and Scooby-Doo. John has also written and drawn for the prestigious Walter Foster Company on four of their "How to Draw" books, including how to draw Superman, Wonder Woman, the DC Heroes, and Batman Beyond.

Dave Cooper has inked for several comic book companies (DC, Marvel, Dark Horse) and on numerous series (Legion of Super Heroes, Valor, Scooby-Doo, and more). He also worked on the original *Batman the Animated Series* style guide. He lives in Bridgewater, NJ.

Terry Beatty's comics credits include the private eye series Ms. Tree and Johnny Dynamite. He continues his lengthy run as inker of DC's animated-style Batman comic books with *The Batman Strikes*. Terry teaches cartooning at the Minneapolis College of Art and Design, and in his "spare time" he paints and sculpts.

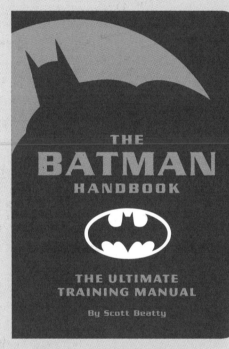